PRAYIN
OUR LORD

WITH
ST. PADRE PIO

EILEEN DUNN BERTANZETTI

FR. BENEDICT J. GROESCHEL, C.F.R.
SERIES EDITOR

Our Sunday Visitor Publishing Division
Our Sunday Visitor, Inc.
Huntington, Indiana 46750

Nihil Obstat
Rev. Michael Heintz
Censor Librorum

Imprimatur
+ John M. D'Arcy
Bishop of Fort Wayne-South Bend
December 13, 2003

The Scripture citations used in this work are taken from the *Catholic Edition of the New Revised Standard Version of the Bible* (NRSV), copyright © 1989 and 1993 by the Division of Christian Education of the National Council of the Churches of Christ in the United States of America. Used by permission.
All rights reserved.

Catechism excerpts are from the English translation of the *Catechism of the Catholic Church, Second Edition,* for use in the United States of America, copyright © 1994 and 1997, United States Catholic Conference — Libreria Editrice Vaticana. Used by permission. All rights reserved.

The author and publisher are grateful to those publishers and others whose materials, whether in the public domain or protected by copyright laws, have been used in one form or another in this volume, including: *Padre Pio of Pietrelcina's Letters, Volumes I, II,* and *III,* copyright © 1985, 1987, 1994, respectively, by San Giovanni Rotondo, used by permission; *Padre Pio: The True Story,* C. Bernard Ruffin, copyright © 1991 by Our Sunday Visitor Publishing Division, used by permission. Every reasonable effort has been made to determine copyright holders of excerpted materials and to secure permissions as needed. If any copyrighted materials have been inadvertently used in this work without proper credit being given in one form or another, please notify Our Sunday Visitor in writing so that future printings of this work may be corrected accordingly.

Our Sunday Visitor Publishing Division
Our Sunday Visitor, Inc.
200 Noll Plaza
Huntington, IN 46750

ISBN: 1-59276-041-4 (Inventory No. T92)
LCCN: 2003113164

Cover design by Tyler Ottinger
Cover art by Robert F. McGovern
Interior design by Sherri L. Hoffman

PRINTED IN THE UNITED STATES OF AMERICA

✠

*To Christ's Virgin Mother Mary,
the Ark of the New Covenant, whose womb first held
the Bread of Life.*

Contents

✠

Foreword

✠

$\mathcal{T}$his collection of meditations drawn from the correspondence of St. Padre Pio is an outstanding addition to our series, *Praying in the Presence of Our Lord*. Anyone familiar with the incredibly moving photographs of Padre Pio in ecstasy at Mass will be fascinated by what he wrote about devotion to Christ in the Eucharist. The extensive collection of Padre Pio's letters can be intimidating because of their volume. We are grateful, then, to the saint's well-known biographer Eileen Dunn Bertanzetti for selecting the best of the great stigmatic's thoughts on Christ's presence in the Holy Eucharist and making them easily available to us.

Carefully assembled and individually introduced, the meditations are enriched by the author with appropriate Scripture quotations. The result is a fine book of meditations, which are summarized by brief but comprehensive prayers. I have found this format very useful in my own book of meditations, and it is very well carried out by Mrs. Bertanzetti. In addition, she has presented a splendid litany to Christ drawn from titles used by St. Pio in his letters and sermons. The author has also provided a collection of the saint's maxims, little jewel-like thoughts to carry with you during the day.

As a lifelong devotee of Padre Pio, I have read many things about him. I agree wholeheartedly with Lutheran Pastor Bernard Ruffin's assessment in *Padre Pio: The True*

Story: "When his total dedication to his faith is considered on the basis of Scripture as well as of Christian tradition, no one can seriously deny that Padre Pio was — and is — one of history's greatest exemplars of Christian humanity."

Padre Pio suffered years of humiliation and temptations that supernatural, or at least inexplicable, phenomena may bring, but he never swerved from his devotion to Christ and the care of souls. I believe that his message of love and devotion to Christ will grow stronger as the necessary Church reforms begin to take place. His life has many prophetic meanings for the Church, but none is more important than that of intimate personal love for Christ, so beautifully brought out in this marvelous collection.

FATHER BENEDICT J. GROESCHEL, C.F.R.

Introduction

✠

During his fifty-eight years as a priest, Padre Pio of Pietrelcina, Italy — proclaimed St. Pio of Pietrelcina by Pope John Paul II on June 16, 2002 — never stopped encouraging the faithful to receive Jesus in the Holy Eucharist and, at every opportunity, to pray in the Presence of Our Lord in the Blessed Sacrament.

In a letter of 1913, St. Pio said, "Never fail to eat the food of the angels."[1] And in his letter of January 4, 1922, he said, "Fly in spirit before the tabernacle when you cannot go there with the body, and there express your ardent desires."[2]

Padre Pio bore the stigmata — the five bleeding wounds of Christ Crucified — for fifty of his fifty-eight years as a priest in Italy. Those wounds never stopped bleeding until shortly before his death in 1968. But even the continual suffering they caused him did not deter him from saying daily Mass — with fervor. Those who attended his Masses witnessed Padre Pio's devotion to Christ in the Holy Eucharist. The intensity on Padre Pio's face and in his voice spoke to each heart and moved souls to repentance.

What transpired inside Padre Pio every time he said Mass? His letter to a priest in 1911 offers a hint: "My heart feels drawn by a higher force each morning before I am united with Him in the Blessed Sacrament. . . ."[3]

Throughout his priesthood, Padre Pio wrote countless letters to people who asked for his guidance. In 1917, he wrote to one such soul, ". . . we must always have courage, and if some spiritual languor comes upon us, let us run to the feet of Jesus in the Blessed Sacrament. . . ."[4]

Though Padre Pio lived in Italy from his birth in 1887 until his death in 1968, people of his era seemed to struggle with many of the things we face today. In 1913, Padre Pio's friend Padre Agostino asked for advice on how to guide a certain troubled soul. Padre Pio wrote to the priest and encouraged him to tell the person "to approach the Eucharistic table daily. . . . The best and only means for her to remain faithful to God — in contact as she is continually with people who know neither faith nor law, who have blasphemy ever on their lips and hatred for God in their hearts — is to receive Jesus every day at the table of the angels."[5]

Who were those people who knew "neither faith nor law," who had "blasphemy ever on their lips and hatred for God in their hearts"? Do they sound like some of today's people we read about in the news, hear about on television, see in movies, and associate with at work and in our neighborhoods?

At times, Padre Pio could feel nothing but amazement and gratitude toward God. In 1915 he wrote, "Give us this day our daily bread, but what bread is this? . . . I recognize primarily the Eucharist. . . ."[6]

Despite Padre Pio's ever-deepening holiness, and despite the many spiritual gifts God gave him to use to help souls — bilocation, conversion, healing, prophecy, reading of souls, the stigmata, and others — Padre Pio always knew well his own weaknesses and sinfulness. In a 1915 letter, he spoke to God, "Ah, Father, I cannot ask

You to remove Jesus from among your people, for I am too selfish; and how could I, who am so weak and half-hearted, live without this Eucharistic food?"[7]

During his eighty-one years, Padre Pio experienced temptations, just like the rest of us. Instead of trying to defeat temptation by his own strength, Padre Pio always sought God's help. To a fellow priest, he explained in 1910, "I weep and moan very much at the feet of Jesus in the Blessed Sacrament on this account [Pio's temptations], and I seem very often to be consoled. . . ."[8]

And in spite of a lifetime of trials of every sort, Padre Pio managed to live a holy life. His secret: "You must never fail to approach the holy Banquet of the divine Lamb, as nothing will better gather your spirit than its King; nothing will warm it so much as its Sun; nothing will dissolve it as sweetly as His Balm. There is no remedy more powerful than this. . . ."[9]

Receive the "Food of the Angels," pray in the presence of Our Lord in the tabernacle, or "fly in spirit" to worship before the Blessed Sacrament when you cannot go there in body. There you will experience God's joy, peace, and — best of all — His overwhelming presence.

About the Meditations: How and Why to Use Them

✠

*T*oday we need something — someone — to help us open up to God and allow God to speak to us in our sorrows, fears, trials, temptations, and even our joys. Like the psalmist in the Old Testament, St. Pio of Pietrelcina — more commonly known as Padre Pio — had the ability to put into words his deepest emotions, senses, and thoughts. And Padre Pio's words of guidance to those who sought his wisdom still hold universal significance, applicable to each of us today.

Take this little book with you when you go before Our Lord in the Blessed Sacrament — or whenever speaking to Jesus, wherever you are — and allow St. Pio's counsel and prayers — like those of the psalmist — become your own. Allow Padre Pio's words to speak to your heart, mind, and soul. You will find God's joy filling you, replacing the darkness, giving you light, enabling you to "pick up your cross daily" — with gratitude — and to follow Jesus.

As St. Pio said, "Do not fear; you are walking on the sea amidst the wind and waves, but you are with Jesus. What is there to fear? But if fear takes you by surprise, pray, 'Oh Lord, save me!' He will stretch out His hand to you.... Squeeze it tightly and walk joyfully...."[1]

PART

I

In the Presence of God

Introduction

*J*ust as he himself did, Padre Pio advised others to "keep Jesus Crucified present to your imagination, in your arms, and on your breast; and kissing His side, say a thousand times, 'This is my hope, the living source of my happiness; this is the Heart of my soul; nothing will ever separate me from God's love. I possess Him and will not leave Him, until He places me in a safe place.'"[1] What better way is there to "keep Jesus Crucified" in your mind, heart, and soul than to spend time with Him in His Real Presence in the Blessed Sacrament?

I

Come to the Bridegroom in His Eucharistic Presence

✠

"It is I, Jesus, who sent my angel to you with this testimony for the churches. I am the root and the descendant of David, the bright morning star."

The Spirit and the bride say, "Come." And let everyone who hears say, "Come." And let everyone who is thirsty come. Let anyone who wishes take the water of life as a gift.

— REVELATION 22:16-17

Padre Pio spent countless hours — from his childhood until the day he died — in the presence of Our Lord in the Blessed Sacrament. He urged everyone to rest in this divine "shadow," too.

ST. PIO'S WORDS

". . . despise the snares of [evil] and, with unlimited trust, sit down in the shadow of the divine Bridegroom and fear nothing. Lucifer's scorching rays will not penetrate the shade of such a densely foliaged tree, and even were they to penetrate it, your soul should not fear to be scorched by them. Those rays which would like to touch you will serve to make you proceed invariably with greater fear and love. So, where the devil intends you to lose, he causes you instead to gain ever-new treasures for Paradise.

"Oh, how well-protected is that soul whom God has gathered beneath His wings. Yes, you can well sit down and rest in utter peace in this shade, for He who fills you with many graces will not allow you to fall. Jesus wants you wholly for himself. . . . Cast yourself with sublime abandonment into the arms of God, and He will fulfill the plans He has for you.

"Consider yourself fortunate to have been made worthy to sit down in the shadow of our Beloved. Drive far from your mind those vain fears . . . because such fears are a genuine waste of time. Do your best, and Jesus will perfect His work in you and be glorified by it."[1]

PRAYER

Christ Our Lord, present in the Most Blessed Sacrament, I hear Your "still, small voice" calling me to come to your Eucharistic Presence, but how easy it is to get caught up in the everyday whirlwind of work, family, and other obligations. How difficult it is to take even a half-hour to spend time with You, meditating on Your Real Presence. Please motivate me to make time to do that. Thank you. Amen.

2

How Exceedingly the Son Loves Us

✠

You show me the path of life. In your presence there is fullness of joy; in your right hand are pleasures forevermore. — PSALM 16:11

Despite his many supernatural gifts from God — which included not only the stigmata, but also healing, prophecy, bilocation, conversions, languages, perfume, and discernment — Padre Pio remained humble. "I am an instrument in divine hands; an instrument which only succeeds in serving some purpose when it is handled by the divine Craftsman. Left to my own devices, I can do nothing but sin, and sin again."[1]

Too often those who receive Christ in the Eucharist do so without even thinking about whom it is they are receiving. If not for the grace of the "divine Craftsman," we, too, would receive Him unworthily.

ST. PIO'S WORDS

"Oh, how exceedingly the Son loves us, and at the same time what excessive humility is His in asking the Father to allow Him to remain with us until the end of the world. Again, what exceeding love has the Father for us, when He has seen Him subjected to such dreadful treatment and still permits this beloved Son of His to remain among us [in the Blessed Sacrament], to be the target of fresh insults every day.

"How could this good Father ever agree to all this? Was it not sufficient, oh eternal Father, to have permitted just once that Your beloved Son should be left a prey to the anger of His enemies? How could You ever agree to His being left among us still, to see Him every day in the unworthy hands of so many dreadful people, worse than his enemies [at Calvary]? How can your most merciful heart, oh Father, bear to see Your only begotten Son so neglected by many unworthy Christians? How can You consent, oh Father, to His being sacrilegiously received by so many unworthy Christians?

"Oh holy Father, how many profanations, how many sacrileges must Your merciful heart still tolerate? Who, then, oh God, is to take up the defense of this most meek Lamb who never opens His mouth to defend himself but speaks on our behalf alone? Ah Father, I cannot ask You now to remove Jesus from among men, for I am too selfish; and how could I who am so weak and half-hearted live without this Eucharistic Food? How could I fulfill that petition made by Your Son in our name: 'Thy will be done on earth as it is in Heaven,' if I did not receive strength from this Immaculate Flesh?"[2]

PRAYER

Lord Jesus, present in the Most Blessed Sacrament, help me to always receive You in the Eucharist, fully aware of Your divine Presence, whole and entire. Help me to accept and appreciate the strength, love, and joy You offer me in Your Immaculate Flesh. Amen.

3
Road to Perfection

╬

"Be perfect, therefore, as your heavenly Father is perfect."
— MATTHEW 5:48

$\mathcal{D}$espite his ever-deepening holiness, Padre Pio always considered himself a "wretched" sinner. He knew that — by his own strength — he could never reach perfection. But, like St. Paul, Padre Pio believed that Christ would save anyone — including Pio the "wretch" — who turned to Him.

ST. PIO'S WORDS

"I think that the Holy Eucharist is a great means through which to aspire to perfection. But we must receive it with the desire and intention of removing from the heart all that is displeasing to He with whom we wish to dwell. Therefore, you must try to continually overcome yourself in those daily struggles which the Lord presents to you. And these efforts must extend also to the constant exercise of correcting your defects, acquiring virtue, and doing good.

"May this be your only desire, and be sure that God wants nothing else from you for the present. . . . Do not scatter the seed in the gardens of others, but cultivate well your own. Don't desire to be anything but what you are; concentrate on perfecting yourself and on carrying the crosses, either small or large, that you will encounter on your journey to Heaven. And believe me that this is the most important advice, but also the least understood in spiritual behavior: Each one loves according to his own tastes. Few, however, live according to their duty and the will of the Lord. From this there arises that tearful state whereby many start out on the path to perfection, but few arrive at the summit of the same perfection."[1]

PRAYER

Christ Our Lord, present in the Most Blessed Sacrament, enable me, through Your Real Presence, to reach the "summit of perfection," in spite of all my weaknesses. For You said that in my weakness You are strong, if I rely on You. Amen.

4

Fly in Spirit

✠

"Come to me, all you that are weary and are carrying heavy bur-
dens, and I will give you rest. Take my yoke upon you, and learn
from me; for I am gentle and humble in heart, and you will find rest
for your souls. For my yoke is easy, and my burden is light."
— MATTHEW 11:28-30

$\mathcal{T}$hough Padre Pio received more than his share of spiritual gifts, he never sought them. He never felt worthy of
them. He never put the gifts before the Giver. About
supernatural gifts, Pio wrote, "…you must by no means
desire such extraordinary things, knowing that it is not
these things that render the soul more perfect, but rather,
holy Christian virtue."[1] And how do we obtain that
virtue? From the real Flesh and Blood of Christ — even
when we cannot, physically, receive the Blessed Sacrament.

ST. PIO'S WORDS

"If you are not granted the ability to stay a long time in
prayer, reading, [or meditating before Christ in the
Eucharist], you must not be discouraged. As long as you

receive Jesus in the Blessed Sacrament every morning, you must consider yourself extremely fortunate.

"During the course of the day, when you are unable to do anything else, call on Jesus, even in the midst of all your occupations, with resigned groanings of the soul. He will come to stay united to your soul always, through His grace and holy love.

"Fly in spirit before the tabernacle when you cannot go there with the body, and there express your ardent desires. Speak to, pray to, and embrace the Beloved of souls, better than if you had been able to receive Him in sacrament."[2]

PRAYER

Lord our God, present in the Blessed Sacrament, when I'm unable to receive You in the Eucharist, please help me to "fly in spirit before the tabernacle" and receive You spiritually. Help me to accept your "yoke" in place of mine and to accept and embrace that "rest" You promise me. Amen.

5
Eternal Tabernacle

✠

"Do not let your hearts be troubled. Believe in God, believe also in me." — JOHN 14:1

*I*n a letter to a troubled friend, Padre Pio wrote, "Call to mind the words the divine Master said to the apostles, and which He says to you today: 'Do not let your hearts be troubled.'"[1]

ST. PIO'S WORDS

"We must always strictly observe these two virtues: sweetness with our neighbors and holy humility with God. I trust you will do this, because the great God who has taken you by the hand in order to draw you to himself, will not abandon you until He has placed you in His Eternal Tabernacle. You should do all that you can to totally uproot pretentiousness and pride. Because the person who never seeks this honor has the greatest honor of all. But [once you reach this stage] this itself could cause you to become proud, making you commit errors against sweetness and humility.

"Take heart in this regard and be patient with yourself when you fall. Do not be at all surprised by distractions and aridity. . . . Do not fail to approach the Lord's altar in similar cases, in order to satiate yourself with the Flesh of the Immaculate Lamb, because nothing will more better reunite the soul than its King; nothing will warm it better than its Sun; and nothing will sweeten it more than His Balm.

"Live humbly, sweet, and in love with our heavenly Bridegroom, and don't worry. . . ."[2]

PRAYER

Lord Jesus Christ, present in the Blessed Sacrament, keep me — and all those I love — safe from evil, dwelling always in the "Eternal Tabernacle" of Your love. Amen.

6
Thy Will Be Done

⨁

"Pray then in this way: Our Father in heaven, hallowed be your name. Your kingdom come. Your will be done, on earth as it is in heaven."

— MATTHEW 6:9-10

On September 20, 1918, while praying in the monastery chapel in San Giovanni, Padre Pio trembled as an angelic being — later identified as the crucified Christ — materialized in front of him. Blood dripped from the being's hands, feet, and side. Terror snaked through Padre Pio at the sight. Then the saint cried out as spears of light, radiating from the being, pierced Padre Pio's hands, feet, and side. The young priest slumped to the floor. Now, as blood dripped from his five fresh wounds, which corresponded to the wounds of the crucified Christ, Padre Pio thought he would surely die.

But he lived, and he continued to trust God and to always say, "Thy will be done."

ST. PIO'S WORDS

"Even now, oh heavenly Father, with the powerful help which Jesus has left us in this Sacrament of Love [the

Eucharist], I often feel I am on the point of wavering and rebelling against Your will. So, what would become of me if I asked You — and You answered my request — to take Jesus [in the Blessed Sacrament] away from the world so that He would not be treated so badly?

"Ah, I lack the strength which I should perhaps have if I loved this most holy Son of yours a little more. But in the meantime, holy Father, I entreat You either to put an end to all the dreadful acts continually committed by people against the adorable Person of Your only begotten Son. Do this, oh Father, since it is in Your power. Do it, because the love this Son has for You calls for such an action on Your part. Glorify Him as He has glorified You and meanwhile, holy Father, give us today our daily bread. Give us Jesus always during our brief stay in this land of exile. Give Him to us and grant that we may be increasingly worthy to welcome Him into our hearts. Yes, give Him to us, and we shall be sure to fulfill the request that Jesus himself addressed to You on our behalf: 'Thy will be done on earth as it is in heaven.'"[1]

PRAYER

Christ Our Lord, present in the Blessed Sacrament, no matter what happens, help me to always say — and mean it — "Thy will be done." Amen.

7
Testing of Faith

✛

My brothers and sisters, whenever you face trials of any kind, consider it nothing but joy, because you know that the testing of your faith produces endurance; and let endurance have its full effect, so that you may be mature and complete, lacking in nothing.

— JAMES 1:2-4

ST. PIO'S WORDS

"...the apostle St. James exhorts souls to rejoice when they see themselves harassed by various temptations, storms, and numerous contradictions.... The reason is because the crown is to be found in the struggle, and the more the soul fights, the more the victories are multiplied. And knowing that, to every victory gained, there corresponds a degree of eternal glory, how can you not rejoice in seeing yourself involved in this task and gaining many victories during the course of your life? May this thought console you, and let the example of our divine Master also encourage you.... In every respect [Jesus] was tempted as we are, yet without sinning, and tempted to the point of being unable to bear it any longer so that He exclaimed, 'My God, my God, why hast thou forsaken me?' [Matthew 27:46]

"Do not listen or pay any attention to what the enemy suggests to you, telling you that God has rejected you, or that because of some hidden failure, God is punishing you and wants to chastise you until you eliminate those things from your soul. This is by no means true. In point of fact, when the soul grieves and fears to offend God, it doesn't offend Him and is very far from doing so. Listen to me who speaks to you in the Lord, telling you that your state of soul is due to your love for God and an incomparable proof of God's love for you."[1]

PRAYER

Dear Christ Jesus, present in the Most Blessed Sacrament, help me to always trust in You — no matter what trials I face — and to believe that Your hand is guiding me and that You will bring good out of my suffering. Amen.

8

Sufficient Grace

✠

Three times I appealed to the Lord about this, that it [the trial] would leave me, but he said to me, "My grace is sufficient for you, for power is made perfect in weakness."

— 2 CORINTHIANS 12:8-9

ST. PIO'S WORDS

"No chosen soul is free from temptations. Not even the apostle [St. Paul] of the people who, after being taken away to Paradise while still a traveling soul, was subjected to such a trial that Satan went so far as to hit him. [2 Corinthians 12:7] Dear God! Who can read those pages without feeling your blood freezing in your veins? How many tears, how many sighs, how many groans, how many prayers did this holy apostle raise, so that the Lord might withdraw this most painful trial from him. But what was Jesus' reply? Only this: 'My grace is sufficient for you, for power is made perfect in weakness.'

"Therefore, take heart. Jesus makes you also hear the same voice He allowed St. Paul to hear…. Fight valiantly and you will obtain the reward of strong souls. Never abandon yourself to yourself. In times of great struggle and prostration, turn to prayer, trust in God, and you will never be overcome by temptation. If the Lord puts you to the test, know that He will not permit this to be beyond your strength. If you are despised by the world, enjoy it, because they first hated the Author of Life, the divine Master. If you are harassed and afflicted with every kind of privation, temptation, and trials by the devil and his followers, raise your eyes on high, redouble your courage. The Lord is with you, and there is no reason to fear."[1]

PRAYER

Lord Jesus, present in the Most Blessed Sacrament, forgive me for not believing — in the middle of my trials — that You are in control, that You will not allow those trials to overcome me. Help me to always believe and trust that, in my weakness, You are strong. Amen.

9

Tried Like Gold

✠

In this [your heavenly inheritance] you rejoice, even if now for a little while you have had to suffer various trials, so that the genuineness of your faith—being more precious than gold that, though perishable, is tested by fire—may be found to result in praise and glory and honor when Jesus Christ is revealed.

— I PETER 1:6-7

ST. PIO'S WORDS

"Calm yourself and be quite certain that these shadows [trials] are not a punishment proportioned to your wickedness. You are not wicked, nor are you blinded by your own malice. You are merely one of the chosen ones who are tried like gold in the furnace. This is the truth, and if I were to say anything else, I would be insincere.

"But what is this painful searching for God which occupies your heart incessantly? It is the effect of the love which draws you and the love which impels you. And why does love take to flight? Because of love and to stimulate love.

"Remember what took place in the heart of our heavenly Mother at the foot of the cross. She was turned to stone before her crucified Son due to the excessive suffering, but you cannot say she was abandoned. On the contrary, she was never loved more than at that moment when she suffered and couldn't even cry. Console yourself and resign yourself to seeing the night falling, without being afraid."[1]

PRAYER

Lord Jesus, truly present in Body, Blood, Soul, and Divinity in the Blessed Sacrament, forgive me for ever doubting that You are always with me. When trials intrude into my life, help me to imagine myself kneeling beside Your most holy Mother at the foot of the cross. There I will know, without a doubt, that You will never abandon me. Amen.

10
Lord, Save Me

✠

One day he [Jesus] got into a boat with his disciples, and he said to them, "Let us go across to the other side of the lake." So they put out, and while they were sailing he fell asleep. A windstorm swept down on the lake, and the boat was filling with water, and they were in danger. They went to him and woke him up, shouting, "Master, Master, we are perishing!" And he woke up and rebuked the wind and the raging waves; they ceased, and there was a calm. He said to them, "Where is your faith?"

— LUKE 8:22-25

ST. PIO'S WORDS

"Let us humble ourselves profoundly and confess that if God were not our breastplate and our shield, we should at once be pierced by every kind of sin. This is why we must invariably keep ourselves in God. . . .

"We must always have courage, and if some spiritual languor comes upon us, let us run to the feet of Jesus in the Blessed Sacrament. Let us place ourselves in the midst of the heavenly perfumes, and we will undoubtedly regain our strength. . . .

"I beg you, for the honor of God, to fear nothing at all, as He doesn't want to do you any harm. Love Him greatly. . . .

"... Don't try excessively to heal your heart, as your efforts would only make it more infirm. Don't make too great an effort to overcome your temptations, as this violence would only make them stronger. Despise them and don't dwell on them too much.

"Keep Jesus Crucified present to your imagination. Hold Him in your arms and on your breast. And, kissing His side, say a thousand times, 'This is my hope, the living source of my happiness; this is the heart of my soul; nothing will ever separate me from His love. I possess Him and will not leave Him, until He places me in a safe place.'

"Often say to Him [in the Blessed Sacrament], 'What can I have on earth, or what can I expect in Heaven, if not You, oh my Jesus? You are the God of my heart and the inheritance I desire for all eternity.'

"Whom should we fear, therefore? Listen to Our Lord who says to Abraham and to you also, 'Do not fear, I am your protector' [Genesis 15:1]. Therefore, be steadfast in your resolutions. Stay in the boat in which He has placed you, and let the storm come. Long live Jesus! You will not perish. He may sleep, but at the opportune time He will awaken to restore your calm."[1]

PRAYER

Lord Jesus, help me to go — either physically or spiritually — to your "feet" in the Blessed Sacrament. There, I will place my fears and worries, my temptations and sins before You. Give me the strength and faith to leave *them there with You and to return to my daily duties, refreshed and strengthened by Your love. Amen.*

II
Holy Banquet of the Divine Lamb

✠

Where can I go from your spirit? Or where can I flee from your presence? If I ascend to heaven, you are there; if I make my bed in Sheol, you are there. If I take the wings of the morning and settle at the farthest limits of the sea, even there your hand shall lead me, and your right hand shall hold me fast.

— PSALM 139:7-10

ST. PIO'S WORDS

"Receive daily Communion, always rejecting unreasonable doubts. . . . Do not fear encountering evil.

"If Jesus manifests himself, thank Him, and if He hides himself, thank Him just the same. All are tricks of love."[1]

"Therefore, live tranquilly. You must not be anxious. . . . You must never fail to approach the holy Banquet of the divine Lamb, as nothing will better gather your spirit than its King; nothing will warm it so much as its Sun; nothing will dissolve it as sweetly as His Balm. There is no remedy more powerful than this.

". . . Live humbly; be docile and in love with your heavenly Spouse. Do not be upset by any infirmities and weaknesses into which you would fall. No, you must not be disturbed by this, because just as we often fall without realizing it, in the same way, without realizing it, we will arise. Scripture doesn't say that the just person sees or feels himself falling seven times a day, but that he falls seven times and, in the same way, without realizing it, he picks himself up.

"Don't upset yourself over this, but humbly and frankly confess before God what you noticed, and place it at the sweet mercy of He who sustains those who fall — without malice — so that they do not suffer any harm. He picks them up so sweetly, they do not realize they have fallen because the hand of God sustained them in their fall. Nor do they realize that they have been picked up, because God did this so quickly, they did not even think of it."[2]

<hr />

PRAYER

Lord Jesus, help me to trust and believe that — no matter what I am doing, whether rejoicing before Your Eucharistic Presence or struggling to carry my cross — You are there. Whether I feel your presence or not, whether I feel happiness or pain, help me to know, without a doubt, that You are with me. Amen.

12
Most Holy Humanity

✠

But you are a chosen race, a royal priesthood, a holy nation, God's own people, in order that you may proclaim the mighty acts of him who called you out of darkness into his marvelous light.

— I PETER 2:9

ST. PIO'S WORDS

"There is a prayer you must never neglect: See how much scorn and sacrilege is committed by men and women toward the Most Holy Humanity of His Son in the Sacrament of Love? It is up to us, as we have been chosen beforehand by the Lord's goodness, to be members of His Church, or as St. Peter says, of a 'royal priesthood.' It is up to us, I repeat, to defend the honor of this meek Lamb who is always concerned when the case of souls is in question, but always silent where His own case is concerned.

"Let our entire lives, our every action and all our aspirations be completely directed toward making reparation for the offenses which our ungrateful brothers and sisters continually do to Him.

"But our thoughts must be raised higher still. There is a Father up there who alone can and must give everything to glorify this most holy Son of His. We must knock at this divine Father's heart, with holy and filial confidence, and pray that He himself will take on the defense of Jesus in the Blessed Sacrament, either by bringing about an end to the world or by stopping so much iniquity."[1]

PRAYER

Lord Jesus, help me, as part of Your "royal priesthood," to make reparation to your Most Holy Presence in the Blessed Sacrament through my every thought, word, and action. In doing so, use me to lead others to a greater respect, love, and devotion to Your Most Holy Humanity. Amen.

13
In the Presence of the Bread of Life

Jesus said to them, "I am the bread of life. Whoever comes to me will never be hungry, and whoever believes in me will never be thirsty."
— JOHN 6:35

You finally have a chance to worship before Jesus, the Bread of Life, truly present in the Sacrament of Salvation. But what do you say to Him? Or should you simply remain silent before Him and let Him speak to your heart and soul? Or should you read from a holy spiritual book to help focus your mind on Christ's presence?

ST. PIO'S WORDS

"Don't worry about not having suitable books from which to take material for holy mental prayers, that is, holy meditation. If Jesus provides you with these books, thank Him for this. If He does not provide you these books, do not be distressed. Any truth of our holy religion can and must be the object of our meditation. The truths of the Christian religion are very, very many, and you know them very well. So be calm and enjoy being a child of Jesus.

"More than anything else, I desire one thing from you in this regard: Your usual meditation should possibly be on the Life — the Passion, Death, Resurrection, and Ascension — of Our Lord Jesus Christ. You could, therefore, meditate on His birth, His flight into and stay in Egypt, His return, His hidden life in the workshop in Nazareth up to the age of thirty, and His humility in having himself baptized by His precursor, St. John. You could also meditate on Christ's public life, His most painful Passion and Death, the institution of the Blessed Sacrament, on that precise evening when men were preparing the most atrocious suffering for Him. You could also meditate on Jesus as He meditated in the olive grove when His sweat became drops of blood at the sight of the suffering which men were preparing for Him, and of the ingratitude of those who would not take advantage of his merits. Meditate on Jesus dragged and beaten in the tribunals; scourged and crowned with thorns; his climb up the hill of Calvary laden with the cross; his crucifixion, and finally, his Death on the cross amidst a sea of anguish at the sight of his most afflicted Mother.

"Yes, there is a great deal of material for meditation, so that books are by no means necessary for our preparation [to adore Christ in the Blessed Sacrament].

"Do not fear the evil snares of the enemy. In the end, he will be obliged to recognize that he is powerless where a soul that is very dear to Jesus is concerned. Therefore be calm."[1]

PRAYER

Lord Jesus, Bread of Life, I am so spiritually hungry and thirsty. Draw me to yourself, let me eat of your eternal life-giving Bread, and let me drink Your "waters of everlasting life," so that I will never hunger and thirst again. Amen.

14
Filial Abandonment

✠

He came down with them and stood on a level place, with a great crowd of his disciples and a great multitude of people. . . . They had come to hear him and to be healed of their diseases; and those who were troubled with unclean spirits were cured. And all in the crowd were trying to touch him, for power came out from him and healed all of them.

— LUKE 6:17-19

ST. PIO'S WORDS

"Enter the church in silence and with great respect, considering yourself unworthy to appear before the Lord's majesty [present in the Sacrament of the Eucharist]. Among other pious considerations, remember that our soul is the temple of God and, as such, we must keep it pure and spotless before God and His angels. Let us blush for having given access to the devil and his snares many times — with his enticements to the world, his pomp, his calling to the flesh — by not being able to keep our hearts pure and our bodies chaste. Let us blush for having allowed our enemies to insinuate themselves into our hearts, thus desecrating the temple of God which we became through holy baptism.

"Then take holy water and make the sign of the cross carefully and slowly. As soon as you are before God in the Blessed Sacrament, devoutly genuflect. Once you have found your place, kneel down and render the tribute of your presence and devotion to Jesus in the Blessed Sacrament. Confide all your needs to Him along with those of others. Speak to Him with filial abandonment, give free rein to your heart, and give Him complete freedom to work in you as He thinks best.

". . . In short, behave in such a way that all present are edified by it and, through you, are urged to glorify and love the heavenly Father."[1]

"Never forget Jesus, this divine Model. Try to see a certain lovable majesty in his Presence [in the Blessed Sacrament]. Try to hear a certain pleasant authority in His manner of speaking [to your heart]. . . . Imagine His extremely composed and sweet expression with which He drew the crowds, making them leave cities and castles, leading them to the mountains, to the forests, and to the solitude of the deserted beaches of the sea. Imagine the crowds totally forgetting food, drink, and their domestic duties in order to follow Him.

". . . Let us do our utmost to be, as far as possible, similar to Him on this earth, in order that we might be more perfect and more similar to Him for the whole of eternity in the heavenly Jerusalem."[2]

". . . On leaving the church, you should be recollected and calm. First, take your leave of Jesus in the Blessed Sacrament by asking His forgiveness for the shortcomings committed in His divine Presence. Last, do not leave Him without asking for and receiving His paternal blessing."[3]

PRAYER

Lord Jesus, draw me to Your Eucharistic Presence and help me to accept Your blessing, Your healing — not necessarily of my body, but certainly of my soul, my spirit, and my heart. Amen.

PART

II

Immaculate Mary: Mother of the Body and Blood of Christ

Introduction

✠

From as early as age five, until his death in 1968, St. Pio experienced daily the reality and love of Christ's Mother. He often had visions of Our Lady, of His holy guardian angel, and of Jesus. Later in his adult life, when asked why he had never told anyone about these visions, St. Pio replied, "I just thought *everyone* had visions." On May 20, 1912, Padre Pio said, "Who could put into writing the consolations which the heavenly Mother makes me feel? . . ."[1] And on May 6, 1913, he said, "What have I done to deserve such delicacy [Mary's maternal care]?"[2]

Even though St. Pio had received many supernatural gifts from God — among them the stigmata and the ability to heal others — he did not consider himself better than anyone else. He continued, ". . . Yet this most tender Mother, in her great mercy, wisdom, and goodness, has . . . poured so many graces into my heart . . . I feel myself held bound to the Son by means of her. . . ."[3]

We do not worship our Blessed Mother, as some accuse us of doing. No, we take Christ at His word when He hung on the cross and said to His Mother, "'Woman, here is your son.' Then he said to the disciple, 'Here is your mother.' And from that hour the disciple took her into his own home" [John 19:26-27]. We, like that disciple, simply seek to take Christ's Mother into our home — into our hearts — because she will never fail to draw us to her divine Son.

With Immaculate Mary at the foot of the cross, with this Queen of all the holy angels and saints before the Blessed Sacrament, let us adore the Sacrifice of the Cross, the Bread of Heaven, the Eucharistic Body and Blood of Jesus, and unite ourselves to Him — through the intercession of His most holy Mother. Believe, as St. Pio did, that this heavenly Mother kneels beside you as you worship her Son in the Blessed Sacrament.

15
One Thing Only

✠

[A] woman named Martha welcomed him [Jesus] into her home. She had a sister named Mary, who sat at the Lord's feet and listened to what he was saying. But Martha was distracted by her many tasks; so she came to him and asked, "Lord, do you not care that my sister has left me to do all the work by myself? Tell her then to help me." But the Lord answered her, "Martha, Martha, you are worried and distracted by many things; there is need of only one thing. Mary has chosen the better part, which will not be taken away from her."
— LUKE 10:38-42

ST. PIO'S WORDS

"Remember that one thing only is necessary: to be close to Jesus. You know well that, at the birth of Our Lord, the shepherds heard the divine and angelic singing of the heavenly spirits. Scripture tells us this, but it does not say that the Virgin, His Mother, and St. Joseph, who were closest to the Infant, heard the voices of the angels or saw those miraculous splendors. On the contrary, instead of hearing the angels singing, they heard the Child crying. They saw, by the light of a poor lamp, the eyes of this divine Infant all wet with His tears and His tiny body trembling from the cold.

"Now I ask you, wouldn't you have chosen to be in that dark stable filled with the cries of the little Child, rather than rejoicing outside with the shepherds at ['the divine and angelic singing of the heavenly spirits']? Yes, undoubtedly you, too, would have exclaimed with St. Peter, 'Lord, it is good for us to be here' [Matthew 17:4].

"... But you are not on Tabor with St. Peter, but on Calvary with Mary, where you see nothing but death, nails, thorns, powerlessness, extraordinary darkness, abandonment, and dereliction. Therefore, I beg you to love the crib of the Child of Bethlehem; love the Calvary of the God crucified amid the darkness; stay close to Him and remember that Jesus is in the midst of your hearts more than you could ever believe or imagine."[1]

PRAYER

Lord Jesus, even when I'm not physically in Your Eucharistic Presence, help me to turn to You and place myself, spiritually, at Your feet. Amen.

16
Enemies Defeated

✠

Discipline yourselves, keep alert. Like a roaring lion your adversary the devil prowls around, looking for someone to devour. Resist him, steadfast in your faith, for you know that your brothers and sisters in all the world are undergoing the same kinds of suffering.

— I PETER 5:8-9

ST. PIO'S WORD

"Our common enemy [the devil] continues to make war on me, and up to the present he has shown no sign of admitting defeat. He wants me to be lost at all costs. He presents to my mind the painful picture of my life and, worse still, tries to lead me to thoughts of despair.

"But I am greatly indebted to our Mother Mary for driving away these temptations of the enemy."[1]

"We must have no illusions about the enemy who is exceedingly strong, if we do not intend to surrender to him. In the light infused by God, the soul understands the great danger to which it is exposed if it is not continually on its guard. The idea of losing all by a possible fall makes my poor soul tremble like a reed in the wind.

"I told you that the strength of Satan, who fights against me, is something terrible, but may God be praised, for Jesus has placed the cause of my salvation and the ultimate victory in the hands of our heavenly Mother. Protected and guided by so tender a Mother, I will continue to fight as long as God wills, full of confidence in this Mother and certain that I will never succumb.

"How far away is the hope of victory, viewed from this land of exile! But how close and certain is the hope of victory, when viewed from God's house, beneath the protection of this most holy Mother."[2]

PRAYER

Lord Jesus, You chose Your Mother Mary to be the first "tabernacle" to hold Your sacred Body and Blood. Help me to remain always beneath the mantle of Mary's love, united to You and protected from all evil. Amen.

17
The Cross

✠

Then Jesus told his disciples, "If any want to become my followers, let them deny themselves and take up their cross and follow me."
— MATTHEW 16:24

ST. PIO'S WORDS

"May Jesus fill your soul with all His choicest graces and enable you to experience more and more the happiness of the cross when carried with a Christian spirit.

"How sweet the word 'cross.' Here, at the foot of Jesus' cross, souls are clothed in light and inflamed with love. Here they acquire wings to bear them upward in loftiest flight.

"May the same cross always be our bed of rest, our school of perfection, our beloved heritage. For this reason we must never separate the cross from Jesus' love, otherwise it would become a weight which, in our weakness, we could not carry.

"May the sorrowful Virgin obtain for us from her most holy Son the grace to penetrate more deeply into the mystery of the cross and, like her, to become inebriated with Jesus' sufferings. The surest sign of love is the capacity to suffer for the beloved, and since the Son of God endured many sufferings for pure love, there is no doubt that the cross, carried for Him, becomes as lovable as love itself.

"May the most holy Virgin obtain for us love of the cross, love of pain and suffering, and may she who was first to practice the Gospel in all its perfection before it was even written, enable us and stimulate us to follow her example.

"We must make every effort, like many elect souls, to follow invariably this blessed Mother, to walk close to her since there is no other path leading to life except the path followed by our Mother. Let us not refuse to take this path, we who want to reach our journey's end.

"Let us invariably unite with this dear Mother and, with her, remain close to Jesus."[1]

"I wish I had a voice strong enough to invite all the sinners of the world to love Our Lady. But since this is not within my power, I have prayed and will pray to my dear holy guardian angel to perform this task for me."[2]

PRAYER

Lord Jesus, help me to always follow the path that Mary — the Mother of your Body and Blood — followed. I know that she will always lead me to You. Amen.

18
Alpha and Omega

✠

Then he said to me, "It is done! I am the Alpha and the Omega, the beginning and the end. To the thirsty I will give water as a gift from the spring of the water of life. Those who conquer will inherit these things, and I will be their God and they will be my children."

— REVELATION 21:6-7

ST. PIO'S WORDS

"May Jesus be always in your mind, in your heart, and before your eyes. May He invariably be your beginning, your continuation, and your end, and may He absorb your entire life into himself. May Jesus' Mother and ours obtain for us from her Son the grace to live a life entirely according to the heart of God, a completely interior life altogether hidden in Him. May this most dear Mother unite us so closely with Jesus that we may never allow ourselves to be enraptured or lured away by anything belonging to this despicable world. May she keep us always close to infinite sweetness, to Jesus. Then alone will we be able to say with St. Paul that we are children of God in the midst of a depraved and corrupt nation."[1]

"May the clement and holy Virgin continue to obtain for you, from the ineffable goodness of the Lord, the strength to sustain, to the end, so many trials of love, which He bestows on you through your increasing mortification. I hope you reach the point of dying with Jesus on the cross, so that you may sweetly exclaim with Him, '*Consummatum est!* It is finished.'"[2]

PRAYER

Lord Jesus, through my frequent reception of Your sacred Body and Blood, through my frequent placing of myself — either physically or spiritually — in your Real Presence in the Blessed Sacrament — absorb me completely into yourself. Amen.

PART

III

The Holy Sacrifice
of the Mass

Introduction

✠

$\mathcal{F}$rom his childhood until his death in 1968, St. Pio's devotion to the Blessed Sacrament and the Mass grew steadily in intensity. Every day during his priesthood, hours before he would say Mass, his hunger for Jesus in the Eucharist grew to an almost unbearable longing. During his Masses, which often lasted up to two hours, Padre Pio would go into ecstasy, and his superior would have to order him to come out of the ecstasy in order to continue the Mass.

After Mass on September 20, 1918, while meditating in the San Giovanni Monastery church, St. Pio received the stigmata, the five bleeding wounds of Christ. Today, the Lord invites all of us to bring our own "bleeding wounds" — both interior and exterior — to Jesus in the Blessed Sacrament.

19
Divine Mercy

✠

While they were eating, Jesus took a loaf of bread, and after bless-
ing it he broke it, gave it to the disciples, and said, "Take, eat; this is
my body." Then he took a cup, and after giving thanks he gave it to
them, saying, "Drink from it, all of you; for this is my blood of the
covenant, which is poured out for many for the forgiveness of sins."
— MATTHEW 26:26-28

ST. PIO'S WORDS

"I can only say that when I am close to Jesus in the
Blessed Sacrament, my heart throbs so violently that it
seems to me, at times, that it will burst out of my chest.

"Sometimes at the altar my whole body burns in an
indescribable manner. My face in particular seems to be
on fire."[1]

"Only God knows what sweetness I experienced after
Mass, so much so that I still feel it. My head and my heart
were burning with a fire which did me good. My mouth
tasted all the sweetness of the Immaculate Flesh of the
Son of God. Oh, at this moment when I still feel almost
all of this sweetness, if I could only bury within my heart
these consolations, I should certainly be in Paradise.

"How happy Jesus makes me. How sweet is His Spirit. But I am confused and can do nothing but weep and repeat, 'Jesus, my Food.' What distresses me most is that I repay all this love of Jesus with so much ingratitude. He continues to love me and to draw me closer to himself. He has forgotten my sins, and I would say that He remembers only His own mercy. Each morning [during Mass], He comes into my poor heart and pours out all the effusions of His goodness. I would like, if it were in my power, to wash with my blood those places in which I committed so many sins. . . . But praised be the mercy of Jesus!"[2]

PRAYER

Lord Jesus, thank you for Your infinite mercy that forgives my sins and protects me from evil. Help me to always throw myself into Your merciful arms and to rest always in Your merciful heart. Amen.

20
You Are God's Chosen One

✠

As God's chosen ones, holy and beloved, clothe yourselves with com-
passion, kindness, humility, meekness, and patience.

— COLOSSIANS 3:12

ST. PIO'S WORDS:

"While I was celebrating Mass, exactly during the Con-
secration, Jesus comforted me. . . ."[1]

"When assisting at holy Mass and the sacred func-
tions, be very composed when standing up, kneeling
down, and sitting. Carry out every religious act with the
greatest devotion. Be modest in your glances; don't turn
your head here and there to see who enters and leaves.
Out of reverence for this holy place, and also out of
respect for those who are near you, don't laugh. Try not to
speak to anybody, except when charity or strict necessity
requests this.

"Once you are outside the church, be as every fol-
lower of [Jesus] the Nazarene should be. Above all, be
extremely modest in everything, as this is the virtue
which, more than any other, reveals the affections of the
heart. Nothing represents an object more faithfully or
clearly than a mirror. In the same way, nothing more

widely represents the good or bad qualities of a soul than the greater or lesser regulation of the exterior, as when one appears more or less modest. You must be modest in speech, modest in laughter, modest in your bearing, modest in walking. All this must be practiced — not out of vanity in order to display yourself, nor out of hypocrisy in order to appear to be good in the eyes of others — but rather for the internal virtue of modesty, which regulates the external workings of the body.

"Therefore [after Mass and always], be humble of heart, mindful of your words, sensible in your resolutions. Always be sparing in your speech, persevering in good reading, attentive in your work, modest in your conversation. . . . Be benevolent toward all. . . .

"Always keep the modesty of the divine Master before your eyes, as an example. . . ."[2]

PRAYER

Lord Jesus, draw me to yourself, fill me with Your Holy Spirit, and enable me to always imitate Your modesty, meekness, humility, kindness, compassion, and patience. In doing so, use me to draw my family, friends, and everyone to You in the Holy Sacrifice of the Mass, and to You who are everywhere — even in my poor heart — at all times. Amen.

21
My Breath, My Life

✠

With great delight I sat in his shadow, and his fruit was sweet to my taste. He brought me to the banqueting house, and his intention toward me was love.

— SONG OF SOLOMON 2:3-4

ST. PIO'S WORDS

"Every day I offer all hearts to God in the holy Sacrifice of the Mass. You, too, must recommend [everyone] . . . to Divine Mercy. . . ."[1]

"Jesus, my breath — my life. Today, trembling, I elevate You in a mystery of love. With You, let me be for the world . . . and for You, a holy priest, a perfect victim."[2]

"Already this morning [during Mass], I began to have a taste of Paradise. And what will it be when we taste it for all eternity?"[3]

"Jesus allows me the comfort of saying Mass every day."[4]

"My heart has found at last a Lover so attached to me that I am incapable of hurting Him anymore. You already know this Lover. He is the One who is never angry with those who offend Him. My heart keeps within itself an infinite number of His mercies. It knows that it doesn't have anything of value with which to glorify itself before Him [on the sacred altar during Mass]. He has loved me and preferred me to many others.

"Whenever I ask Him what I have done to deserve such consolations, He smiles and says repeatedly that nothing is refused to such an intercessor. In return, He asks me for nothing but love, but do I not perhaps owe Him this out of gratitude?

"If only I could make Him happy just as He makes me happy. He is so much in love with my heart that He makes me burn with His divine fire, with the fire of His love. What is this fire that pervades my whole being? If Jesus makes us so happy on earth, what will Heaven be like?

"I often ask myself if any people exist who do not feel their breast burning with divine fire, especially when they are close to Him in the Blessed Sacrament. This seems impossible to me. . . . Perhaps those who say they do not feel this fire [during Mass] do not notice it because their hearts are bigger [than mine].

". . . I cannot help abandoning myself to this tenderness, this happiness. . . . I trust Jesus so completely, that even if I were to see hell open before me and find myself on the brink of the abyss, I should not lose confidence. I should not despair but continue to trust in Him."[5]

PRAYER

Lord Jesus, You are truly the Lover of my heart, my soul, my all. Help me to always be faithful to that love and to trust You in all situations. Help me to appreciate, worship, and love Your Most Holy Presence in the Eucharist. Amen.

22
In Paradise with the Divine Prisoner

He [Jesus] replied, "Truly I tell you, today you will be with me in Paradise."

— LUKE 23:43

ST. PIO'S WORDS

"Praise be to Jesus. . . . How am I to tell you about the new triumphs of Jesus in my soul? . . . What a burning fire I felt in my heart [during Mass]. But I also felt that this fire was lit by a friendly hand, by a divinely jealous hand. . . .

"When Mass was over, I remained with Jesus in thanksgiving. Oh, how sweet was the colloquy with Paradise that morning. It was such that, although I want to tell you all about it, I cannot. There were things which cannot be translated into human language without losing their deep and heavenly meaning. The heart of Jesus and my own — allow me to use the expression — were fused. No longer were two hearts beating, but only one. My own heart had disappeared, as a drop of water is lost in the ocean. Jesus was its Paradise, its King. My joy was so intense and deep that I could bear no more, and tears of happiness poured down my cheeks.

"Yes, some cannot understand that when Paradise is poured into a heart, this afflicted, exiled, weak, and mortal heart cannot bear it without weeping. I repeat that it was the joy that filled my heart which caused me to weep for so long.

"This visit, believe me, restored me completely. Praise be to the divine Prisoner!"[1]

PRAYER

Lord Jesus, when I receive Your Body and Blood — the divine Prisoner — in the Eucharist, remind me that wherever You are — even within my poor body and soul — there is Paradise. Amen.

PART

IV

Eucharistic Meditations on Guardian Angels; on God the Father, Son, and Holy Spirit; and on Heaven

Introduction

✠

*I*n one of St. Pio's letters, he said, ". . . live tranquilly and don't be bewildered in the dark night through which your spirit is passing. Be patient and resigned while awaiting the return of your divine Sun, which will soon come to brighten the forest of your spirit."[1]

Why did St. Pio have such undying confidence in Christ? Through his own experiences with poverty, health problems, emotional pain, and other trials, he learned to "take heart; it is Jesus who permits your soul to be in a state of . . . darkness. . . . The Lord wants to lead you amidst the thorns because He wants you to be similar to Him."[2]

While the media and our culture try to force us to believe that we have to avoid all suffering at all cost, because there is no value or purpose to our suffering, we must "take heart," as St. Pio said. By accepting our daily crosses and following in the bleeding footsteps of Our Lord, by meditating before His Real Presence in the Blessed Sacrament, we become more like Him, we atone for sin, we intercede for others, and we eventually reach that heavenly homeland where suffering no longer exists.

Today, go to Jesus — either physically or spiritually — the living Bread of Heaven, truly present in every tabernacle throughout the world, and place your trials and sorrows, and your spiritual, emotional, and physical sufferings before Him. There you will find the strength to pick up your cross again and follow Jesus, but now in peace, knowing He will help you shoulder your burdens and thereby make them all joy.

23
With Your Good Angel, Sing Praises

✠

Then I looked, and I heard the voice of many angels surrounding the throne ... singing with full voice, "Worthy is the Lamb that was slaughtered to receive power and wealth and wisdom and might and honor and glory and blessing!"

— REVELATION 5:11-12

St. Pio relied on his guardian angel to help him in everything, including resisting temptation and getting to Mass on time. Our guardian angels are gifts from God to assist us in reaching our heavenly homeland. They receive great joy in accompanying us in prayer before the Real Presence of Our Lord in the Blessed Sacrament. How long can you rely on your guardian angel's constant help? St. Pio said, "... from the cradle to the grave." Trust your guardian angel to aid you in all of your efforts to lead a holy life, including in your efforts to worship and honor Christ's Body and Blood present in the Blessed Sacrament.

ST. PIO'S WORDS

"Again at night when I close my eyes, the veil is lifted, and I see Paradise open up before me. Gladdened by this vision, I sleep with a smile of sweet beatitude on my lips and a perfectly tranquil countenance, waiting for the little companion of my childhood [his guardian angel] to come to waken me, so that we may sing together the morning praises to the Beloved of Our Hearts."[1]

"May your good angel be your breastplate to ward off the blows that the enemies of our salvation aim at you. How consoling it is to know you are always under the protection of a heavenly spirit who never abandons you, not even when you are actually offending God. How delightful is this great truth to the one who believes. Who is to be feared, then, by the devout soul who is trying to love Jesus, when accompanied by such an illustrious warrior? Was your angel not, perhaps, one of the multitude who joined with St. Michael in the Heavens to defend God's honor against Satan and against all the other rebellious angels, to vanquish them in the end and drive them down to hell [see Revelation 12:7-9]?

"Well, then, let me tell you that your guardian angel is still powerful against Satan and his evil satellites. His [your angel's] love has not lessened, and he can never fail to defend you. Make a habit of thinking of him continually. The fact that we have close to us an angelic spirit who never leaves us for an instant — from the cradle to the grave — who guides and protects us like a friend or brother or sister, must fill us with consolation, especially in our more dreary moments."[2]

PRAYER

Lord Jesus, thank you for assigning to me my guardian angel. Help me to always trust You — through my angel — to guide and guard me and to lead me to Your most glorious Presence in the Blessed Sacrament. Amen.

24
Bread of Angels

[H]e rained down on them manna to eat, and gave them the grain of heaven. Mortals ate of the bread of angels.

— PSALM 78:24-25

"I am the living bread that came down from heaven. Whoever eats of this bread will live forever; and the bread that I will give for the life of the world is my flesh. . . . This is the bread that came down from heaven, not like that which your ancestors ate, and they died. But the one who eats this bread will live forever."

— JOHN 6:51, 58

*I*n a letter of June 26, 1913, Padre Pio wrote, "Never fail to eat the food of the angels."[1] Who better to help you follow this advice than your own guardian angel?

ST. PIO'S WORDS

"I turned to my angel [in my suffering], and after he had kept me waiting a while, there he was, hovering close to me, singing hymns to the divine Majesty in his angelic voice. . . . I rebuked him bitterly for having kept me waiting so long when I had not failed to call him to my assistance. . . . But he, poor creature . . . almost in tears, held me until I raised my eyes to his face and found him all upset. Then he said, 'I am always close to you, hovering around you with the affection aroused by your gratitude to the Beloved of your heart. This affection of mine [for you] will never end, not even when you die. I know that your generous heart beats all the time for the One we both love. You would cross every mountain and every desert in search of Him, to see Him again, to embrace Him again in these extreme moments, and to ask Him to break at once this chain which unites you to the body . . . that far from Him you may no longer suffer so much, that He take you to himself. Tell Him that, separated from Him, you reap more sorrow than joy. This is precisely the gift you want from Him, but do not grow weary . . . you must wait a little longer. . . . But do not cease to ask Him insistently for this because His supreme delight is to have you with Him. And although He cannot yet satisfy you, since providence wills that you remain in exile [in this earthly life] a little longer, He will gratify you in the end. . . .'

"Poor little angel," continued Padre Pio. "He is too good. Will he succeed in making me appreciate the serious duty of gratitude?"[2]

PRAYER

Lord Jesus, thank you for Your Body and Blood — the Food of the angels, our Food. Help me always to show my gratitude for Your mercy and grace, which radiate from Your divine Presence in the Blessed Sacrament. Amen.

25

In the Garden and on the Cross with Jesus

Then he said to them, "I am deeply grieved, even to death; remain here, and stay awake with me."

— MATTHEW 26:38

St. Pio had the gift of healing, and millions of pilgrims flocked to his San Giovanni monastery to receive healing, from God, through Pio. Though not every pilgrim who sought physical healing received one, most — perhaps all — pilgrims left San Giovanni having received the most important healing: that of their souls and spirits. St. Pio most often advised pilgrims, as well as all who wrote letters to him, to *accept* their sufferings and to offer them to Jesus for the salvation of souls — including for the souls of the ones *doing* the suffering. The world's attitude toward suffering has not changed since Padre Pio's death in 1968. But the Lord's plea for us to "remain" with Him and to "stay awake" with Him by meditating on His Passion and on His Body and Blood in the Blessed Sacrament has not changed either.

"I complained to my guardian angel [about my trials], and after giving me a little sermon, he said, 'Thank Jesus who is treating you as one chosen to follow Him closely up the steep ascent of Calvary. Oh Pio, soul confided by Jesus to my care, I behold with joy and deep emotion this behavior of Jesus toward you. Do you perhaps think I should be so happy if I did not see you ill-treated like this? I who in holy charity greatly desire your good, rejoice more and more to see you in this state. Jesus permits these assaults of the devil, because Jesus' compassion makes you dear to Him, and He wants you to resemble himself in the torments He endured in the desert, in the garden and on the cross.'

"My guardian angel continued, 'Defend yourself, Pio. Always reject and despise the devil's evil insinuations, and when your own strength is not sufficient, do not be distressed, beloved of my heart, for I am close to you.'"

Days later, St. Pio said to a human friend, "What have I ever done to deserve such exquisite kindliness on the part of my angel? But I do not worry. Isn't the Lord free to bestow His graces on whomever He wills and in the way that pleases Him? I am the plaything of the Child Jesus, as He tells me frequently, but what is worse, Jesus has chosen a toy of no value whatever."[1]

"May your good guardian angel always watch over you; may he be your guide on the bitter paths of life. May he always keep you in the grace of Jesus and sustain you with his hands so that you may not stumble on a stone. May he protect you under his wings from all the snares of the world, the devil, and the flesh."[2]

PRAYER

Lord Jesus, I thank You for helping me to understand and believe that my sufferings — when freely offered to You — can become prayers to our heavenly Father, prayers that can help save many souls, including my own. Keep my heart and soul "awake" always to Your ongoing suffering in Your children. And help me to "remain" with You, spiritually, in Your Real Presence in the tabernacle. Amen.

26

Our Most Sweet Lover

And Mary said, "My soul magnifies the Lord, and my spirit rejoices in God my Savior...."

— LUKE 1:46-47

Some believe that Christ's Mother Mary was the first person to bear the spiritual stigmata, the invisible wounds of Christ. From the moment the angel appeared to her and announced that she had been chosen by God to bear His Son, Mary chose to bear all the sufferings associated with such a "calling." Like any mother, whenever her baby suffered, Mary suffered. Whenever He was threatened — by Caesar, Pilate, or the crowds, or even by his disciple Judas Iscariot — Mary suffered, too. Imagine how she grieved beneath Christ's cross as the Precious Blood dripped from His sacred wounds. The innocent One she had so tenderly loved and cared for all those years was dying on the cross for our sins.

Yet her Son — God's only begotten Son — gave her the graces necessary to humbly accept the Father's will and to find a measure of gratitude, peace, hope, and even joy in her sufferings, knowing that the sacrifice of her Son would redeem the world. Throughout her life, therefore,

Mary was able to continue to say, "My soul magnifies the Lord, and my spirit rejoices in God my Savior."

ST. PIO'S WORDS

"What soul, to whom Jesus has given himself as its inheritance, can be unhappy? Is He not the same Jesus who is the delight of the angels and the only object of the heavenly Father's pleasure? Therefore you are right to say you are well with Jesus. May He be blessed forever that, in the midst of a corrupt nation, He desires to draw us to His love. Let all creatures praise Him with one voice, and may their praise be eternal as He himself is eternal. May our souls always rejoice with happiness. . . . Let us spend our whole lives giving thanks to the divine Father who, in an excess of love for us, sent His only begotten Son and our most sweet Lover. Protected, covered, and defended by the Presence of this dear Lord, let us stand before Him [in the Blessed Sacrament] and pray with the humility of the creature and the confidence and freedom of the child. And given that He loves to delight in His children, let nothing in the world distract us from delighting in Him, contemplating His grandeur and infinite titles, by which He has a right to our praises and love. Let us pray to Him that He be generous as usual, with His divine help, so that, through us, His holy name may be greatly praised and blessed. So that we, too, can say in truth, with our heavenly Mother, 'My soul magnifies and praises the Lord.'"[1]

PRAYER

Lord Jesus, help me to accept my sufferings and to always find, like Mother Mary, a measure of gratitude, peace, hope, and even joy in my own sufferings, knowing that — in some mysterious way that only You fully understand — my suffering, when freely offered up, will act as prayers of intercession for the salvation of many souls, including my own. Amen.

27

Invitation, Gaze, and Medicine of the Holy Trinity

"No one can come to me unless drawn by the Father who sent me; and I will raise that person up on the last day. It is written in the prophets, 'And they shall all be taught by God.' Everyone who has heard and learned from the Father comes to me . . . whoever believes has eternal life. I am the bread of life."

— JOHN 6:44-48

When you physically — or spiritually — visit Christ in the Blessed Sacrament, you do so at the invitation of God the Father who draws you to His Son. In the presence of the Bread of Life, and under His loving gaze, you will find forgiveness, comfort, strength, and peace.

ST. PIO'S WORDS

"If you happen to commit a sin, don't lose heart at all. . . . Continue to serve this infinite goodness of the heavenly Father with ever-increasing sincerity and sweetness of spirit, because, with much love and sweetness, He has invited and called you to himself."[1]

"Jesus is with you and is pleased with your soul, and you love and serve Him carefully and faithfully without being aware of it. You do not offend the Lord at all, but you love Him greatly, and precisely because you love Him, the Lord has rested His gaze of superlative pleasure on you. He holds you dear, and it is precisely for this reason that He subjects you to all the suffering of His painful Passion. Therefore, your state is admirable from all aspects. Be resigned and comforted. . . ."[2]

"As regards your soul, once again I want to assure you, on behalf of the Lord, to fear nothing. God has rested His gaze on you, and He wants to treat you as a chosen soul, allowing you to experience the most bitter and harsh trials, so that you, too, can participate, by your voluntary sacrifice, in helping to make up for what is lacking in the Passion of Christ, in accordance with the apostle's words [see Colossians 1:24].

"You are suffering and are right to complain. By all means complain and in a loud voice, but fear nothing. The Victim of Love [Christ in the Blessed Sacrament] is impatient to possess you. You must cry out that you can take no more and that it is impossible to resist the treatment of the Beloved who wants you and leaves you and leaves you while He wants you."[3]

"Consider yourself to be absolutely nothing before the Lord, and always have great veneration for everybody, but especially for those who love God. . . ."[4]

"Do not give too much importance to what the enemy and your imagination suggest to you regarding your interior suffering and spiritual aridity, being sure that this is best for you. Lovingly and sweetly make this resolution: either to die spiritually or be cured. And as you don't want to die spiritually, try to be healed perfectly. In order to be healed, desire to bear the treatment and correction of the Divine Doctor [the Holy Spirit]. Beseech Him not to spare you in anything in order to save you.

"God has shown great mercy toward you by placing you in this present state of spiritual aridity, in order that, before Him, you might be stripped of everything except God."[5]

PRAYER

Lord Jesus, sometimes, when I'm in the "state of spiritual aridity," I don't even feel like praying, and I certainly do not feel Your presence. I wonder how You — the Bread of Life — could ever love me, a miserable sinner. Help me to accept my weak humanity and to bow always humbly before You and accept the "medicine" of Your Holy Spirit who longs to heal my heart and soul. Amen.

28
Open the Door

✠

"Listen! I am standing at the door, knocking; if you hear my voice and open the door, I will come in to you and eat with you, and you with me."

— REVELATION 3:20

*H*ave you ever wanted to "open the door" of your heart for Jesus, and yet, at the same time, you could not believe that this great and good God of all creation would ever want to dwell within your miserable, weak self? Even great saints, such as St. Pio, knew they could never be good enough to deserve — at least on this earth — the presence of Jesus in their poor hearts. But, at the same time, they realized that, in His great love for us, God wants to dwell within each of us, making us part of His kingdom.

In prayer, before the Blessed Sacrament, you can open the door to your heart and experience the never-ending peace and joy your Guest will bring with Him.

ST. PIO'S WORDS

"...place yourself in the presence of God, humbling your-self profoundly at the thought of whom you are and to whom you are presenting yourself. Ask God for the grace to perform well the mental prayers you are about to practice, in order that you may obtain the fruit that God wants from it. Recommend yourself to the most holy Virgin's intercession, along with the entire heavenly court's, that they may help you to meditate well and keep all distractions and temptations far from you.

"Once you have done this, begin your meditation [on the Life, Passion, and Death of Our Lord Jesus].... Ask God for all the grace and help you need. Recommend all people to the Lord, both in general and in particular. Pray for the reestablishment of God's reign; for the propagation of the faith; for the exaltation and triumph of our holy mother, the Church. Pray for the living, the dead, for the unfaithful, for heretics, and for the conversion of sinners.

"Once you have done all this, offer God your meditation and prayers, along with the offering of your entire self and all those people who are dear to you. Offer everything to God along with the merits of Jesus and of His — and our — Mother. And offer all of this through the hands of most holy Mary, through your good guardian angel, through St. Joseph, and....

"Finally, make a brief examination of how you behaved during this meditation. When you see your defects, humble yourself before God, asking His pardon and proposing to make amends....

"If you want to become perfect, always keep present in your mind what God said to Abraham: 'Walk before me, and be blameless' [Genesis 17:1]. It is true that, given our condition, it is not within our power to keep our thoughts always fixed on God, but let us do our best to keep ourselves, as far as possible, in His presence. This we can and must do, calling to mind every now and then, the great truth: God sees us. . . .

"Live calmly and do not worry excessively, because in order to work more freely within us, the Holy Spirit needs tranquillity and calm. And for you, every anxious thought is a mistake, as you have no reason to fear. It is the Lord who works within you, and you must do nothing except leave the door of your heart wide open so that He might work as He pleases."[1]

PRAYER

Lord Jesus, help me to listen for Your knock. Help me to quiet myself enough to hear that knock, to open the door of my heart, and to allow You to reign in my heart as my King, forever and ever. Amen.

29
No Winter in Heaven or Your Heart

[God] my beloved speaks and says to me: "Arise, my love, my fair one, and come away; for now the winter is past, the rain is over and gone. The flowers appear on the earth; the time of singing has come...."

— SONG OF SOLOMON 2:10-12

You long for Heaven, where there will be no winter to endure — either physically or spiritually. While on this earth, when the harshness of the winter of your soul threatens to steal your faith, peace, and joy, flee — either physically or in spirit — to Christ in the Blessed Sacrament. There He will comfort you with the assurance that it is God who allows those "winters" of yours in order to make you more like His Son so that, one day, you will share the eternal spring with Him in Heaven.

ST. PIO'S WORDS

"Humble yourself before God ... pray in the silence of your heart ... and you will one day enjoy our Beloved in a torrent of never-ending delights [in Heaven]."[1]

"All the seasons of the year can be found in your soul. Sometimes you feel the winter of so much sterility, distraction, listlessness, and boredom. Sometimes you experience the dews of the month of May with the perfume of holy little flowers [good deeds and penances]. Sometimes you experience the colors of the desire to please God. Nothing remains but the autumn, which, as you see, does not bear too much fruit. But it often happens that, when the grain is threshed and the grapes crushed, you find the harvest is greater than it had promised.

"You would like it to be eternally spring and summer. But no, these rotations are necessary, both internally and externally. Only in Heaven will everything be spring as regards beauty; autumn as regards enjoyment; and summer as regards love. There will be no winter, but here winter is necessary in order to practice self-denial and those beautiful little virtues which are practiced in time of sterility."[2]

PRAYER

Lord Jesus, during my interior "winters," help me turn to You in prayer so that You can teach me to use the bleakness of those winters to draw me closer to You. And teach me to be grateful even for those winters. Amen.

30
Within You

✛

"The kingdom of God is not coming with things that can be observed; nor will they say, 'Look, here it is!' or 'There it is!' For, in fact, the kingdom of God is within you."

— LUKE 17:20-21

*I*f you have received Christ — either physically in Holy Communion or spiritually through prayer — the kingdom of God is within you.

ST. PIO'S WORDS

"Always live tranquilly, as regards your spirit, because God reigns there as supreme King. Always keep present to your mind this truly excellent lesson which deserves to be understood well: This present life is given to us in order to acquire the eternal, and due to a lack of reflection, we base our affections on that which pertains to this world through which we are passing, so that when we have to leave it, we are frightened and agitated. Believe me, in order to live happily while on pilgrimage [on earth], we must keep before our eyes the hope of arriving at our Homeland where we will stay for eternity. In the meantime, we should believe this firmly, because given that it is God who calls us to himself, He watches how we make our way to Him, and He will never permit anything to happen to us that is not for our greater good. He knows what we are, and He will extend His paternal hand to us while we are going through rough stretches, so that nothing will prevent us from running quickly to Him. But in order to receive this grace, we must have total confidence in Him."[1]

PRAYER

Lord Jesus, help me to spend more time in Your Real Presence, meditating on the fact that You dwell within me and have established Your kingdom there. Help me to place myself spiritually in Your presence throughout the day, putting all my confidence in You so that I fear nothing, not even death. Amen.

31
Troubles Can Help You

✠

We know that all things work together for good for those who love God, who are called according to his purpose.
— ROMANS 8:28

For fifty years, Saint Pio bore the stigmata, the five wounds of Christ, and even though those wounds never stopped bleeding or hurting, Padre Pio accepted his pain as a gift from God, a gift that would help Jesus to save souls. Though he only wanted to live a quiet, hidden life in the monastery in San Giovanni, his stigmata drew millions to him, causing the shy Padre Pio much humiliation and stress. Yet he bore it all with patience, love, and joy — for Jesus and for the salvation of souls. And he did all this by God's grace, which he received by spending as much time as he could each day in prayer, many hours of that in the presence of the Blessed Sacrament.

ST. PIO'S WORDS

"Do not anticipate the problems of this life with apprehension, but rather with a perfect hope that God, to whom you belong, will free you from them in due time. Hasn't He defended you up until now? Simply hold tightly to the hand of His divine providence, and He will help you in all events, and when you are unable to walk, He will assist you. Don't worry. Why should you fear when you belong to this God who strongly assures us: 'We know that all things work together for good for those who love God, who are called according to his purpose' [Romans 8:28]?

"Don't think about tomorrow's events because the same heavenly Father who takes care of you today will do the same tomorrow and forever. Oh, He will not harm you, and if He allows troubles to come to you, He will grant you invincible courage to bear them.

"Live tranquilly, remove from your imagination that which upsets you, and often say to Our Lord, 'Oh God, you are my God, and I will trust in You. You will assist me and be my refuge, and I will fear nothing,' because not only are you *with* Him, but you are *in* Him, and He is within you. What can a child fear in the arms of its father? Be like children; they almost never think about their future, as they have somebody to think of it for them. They are only strong enough when they are with their parents. Therefore, you do the same and you will be in peace."[1]

PRAYER

Lord Jesus, my strength comes from You, the Bread of Life. You told St. Paul that it is because of our weaknesses that You can be strong within us. Lord, be the strength of my life. You know my weaknesses and how I often fear that my troubles will overcome — even destroy — me, mentally, physically, and spiritually. Give me courage to face my trials and fears. Give me confidence — not in my weak self — but in You who are my strength. Amen.

32
Even on Earth, Simply Love God

✠

"Teacher, [one of the Pharisee lawyers said to Jesus], which com-
mandment in the law is the greatest?" [Jesus] said to him, "You shall
love the Lord your God with all your heart, and with all your soul,
and with all your mind. This is the greatest and first commandment."
— MATTHEW 22:36-38

Within the dark interior of the tabernacle, Jesus humbly
hides from your body's eyes. Yet your faith enables your
soul to "see" Him. Your soul flies to Him, embraces Him.
You become one with the Trinity in whose image you
were made. Your Heaven begins on earth, in your soul.

ST. PIO'S WORDS

"The desire to be in eternal peace is good and holy, but
you must moderate that desire with complete resignation
to divine will. It is better to do divine will on earth, than
to enjoy Paradise. To suffer and not to die was St. Teresa's
motto. Purgatory is sweet when you suffer for love of
God.

"The trials to which the Lord is subjecting you at
present, and those trials to which He will subject you in
the future, are all evidence of divine love, and jewels for

the soul. The winter will pass, and the never-ending spring [Heaven] will come, all the richer in beauty because the storms [you endured] were strong. The darkness you are experiencing is an indication of the closeness of God to your soul.

"Moses, that great leader of the people of God, found the Lord in the darkness of Sinai. The Jewish people saw Him in the form of a cloud, and He appeared in the Temple as a cloud also. Jesus Christ, in the transfiguration on Mt. Tabor, was first visible, and then He rendered himself invisible to His apostles because He was covered by a shining cloud. When God hides himself in the darkness, He is actually making himself more clear to your gaze. From His being visible and intelligible, He becomes transfigured into the purely divine.

"The struggle with the enemy must not frighten you. The more God becomes intimate with your soul, the more the adversary fights in an interior manner. Have courage, therefore.

"As regards the shadows that seem to thicken within you: They are not shadows, but light, and such a strong light that it astonishes the soul, which is accustomed to thinking of God in the usual, almost-human manner. Thank the Lord for having allowed you to foretaste, from this life, that vision [Heaven] in which, when nothing is seen, everything is seen."[1]

"May God bless you so that you may persevere in the task of always keeping the most precious affection of your heart for Him alone. How happy you will be in this miserable life, because in this way, the end of it will be the holy beginning of a beautiful and holy eternity.

"Furthermore, try to always guard these two virtues in your heart: sweetness toward your neighbor and loving humility toward God. And I hope you will succeed in this, because this God, who has taken you by the hand in order to bring you to himself, will never abandon you until you are assured of His Eternal Tabernacle."[2]

PRAYER

Heavenly Father, thank you for allowing Jesus to remain with us, not only hidden in every tabernacle around the world, but hidden in my poor heart as well. Help me to spend my life on earth — and my eternal life in Heaven — keeping, as St. Pio said, "the most precious affection of my heart for You alone." Amen.

PART

V

The Beauty of
Christ Crucified

Introduction

✠

*F*rom 1918 until just before his death in 1968, in addition to suffering the humiliation and physical pains caused by the ever-bleeding stigmata, Padre Pio also suffered spiritual trials. But he knew that Christ could — in some mysterious way—use all of his sufferings to save souls, if Padre Pio only accepted them and offered them up to God. In that way, his sufferings became like prayers for the conversion of sinners and the salvation of souls — even for the souls of the dearly departed. Padre Pio often advised others, "As regards your usual trials . . . I recommend calm and resignation, always, to divine will. . . . Jesus glorified is beautiful; but even though He is such in that state, He seems to me to be even more beautiful crucified."[1]

In saying this, Pio was encouraging others to imitate St. Paul when the apostle said, "I am now rejoicing in my sufferings for your sake, and in my flesh I am completing what is lacking in Christ's afflictions for the sake of His body, that is, the Church" [Colossians 1:24].

According to author C. Bernard Ruffin, Padre Pio believed in the "doctrine of co-redemption, maintaining that salvation, among other things, involves sharing Christ's grief and pain for the sake of one's own salvation and that of others. [Padre Pio] indicated that Christ's 'desolate heart has need of comfort' and that one of the duties of being a Christian is sharing Christ's bitterness and mortal anguish."[2]

Even though Padre Pio believed that all Christians should voluntarily offer up their sufferings to God, in atonement for their own sins and for the sins of the world, Christ used St. Pio to heal many — though not all — of the millions of people who sought physical healing from the stigmatized priest of San Giovanni. Why didn't God heal *all* of their physical ailments? The Church offers this reasoning: "The Holy Spirit gives to some [like Padre Pio] a special charism of healing so as to make manifest the power of the grace of the Risen Lord. But even the most intense prayers do not always obtain the healing of all illnesses. Thus St. Paul must learn from the Lord that 'my grace is sufficient for you, for my power is made perfect in weakness,' and that the sufferings to be endured can mean that 'in my flesh I complete what is lacking in Christ's afflictions for the sake of His Body, that is, the Church.'"[3]

What troubles are you facing? By offering them to Jesus, you can help Him save the souls of others as well as your own soul.

33

Remain in the Darkness of His Passion

He [Jesus] was despised and rejected by others; a man of suffering. . . . Surely he has born our infirmities . . . he was wounded for our transgressions, crushed for our iniquities; upon him was the punishment that made us whole, and by his bruises we are healed.

— ISAIAH 53:3-5

St. Pio asked those who sought his help to offer their pain to God the Father, in union with His suffering Son's Passion. Padre Pio specifically encouraged these souls to offer their pain to God in the Blessed Sacrament.

ST. PIO'S WORDS

"I know you are suffering, but isn't this suffering a sure sign that God loves you? Isn't this suffering perhaps the mark of those who have chosen a crucified God as their inheritance? I know your spirit is always clothed in the darkness of the trial, but suffice it for you to know that Jesus is with and in you.

"Therefore, beware of complaining that you are a miserable and unhappy creature, because besides the fact that those expressions are unseemly for a servant of God, they are born in an excessively dejected heart and are nothing but impatience and resentment."[1]

"Always remember that the Lord is totally yours. What does He ask of you in return? Let us leave this answer to the saint of Chiaravalle, St. Bernard, who said, 'He who has given all, seeks all.' Well, this God is content with such a small offering. Belong entirely to Him. Let nothing prevent you from abandoning yourself totally into the arms of His divine providence. Therefore, remain there, in the darkness of the Passion. Don't let those impure thoughts which cloud your mind frighten you. Despise them always, without becoming discouraged or tired. Live with your thoughts always fixed on God, and you will never be overcome."[2]

PRAYER

Heavenly Father, remind me, in my sufferings, that they are gifts from You that somehow — in some mysterious way — are used by You to save my soul and the souls of others. Keep me always at the foot of the cross, meditating on Christ's Passion, and uniting my own sufferings to His. Remind me that, in the shadow of the darkness of the Passion, before You in the Eucharist, I will find the light of Christ. Amen.

34
Victim of Divine Love

✠

Beloved, do not be surprised at the fiery ordeal that is taking place among you to test you, as though something strange were happening to you. But rejoice insofar as you are sharing Christ's sufferings, so that you may also be glad and shout for joy when his glory is revealed.

— I PETER 4:12-13

Why do our daily lives never fail to bring a measure of suffering to us and to those we love? Why does a loving God allow it?

ST. PIO'S WORDS

"I do not know what will happen to me; I only know one thing for certain, that the Lord will never fall short of His promises. 'Do not fear,' Jesus tells me continually. 'I will let you suffer, but I will also give you the strength to suffer. I want your soul to be purified and tried by a daily hidden martyrdom. Do not be frightened if I allow . . . the world to disgust you and your nearest and dearest to afflict you, for nothing will prevail against those who groan beneath the cross for love of me and those whom I have taken care to protect. How many times,' said Jesus to me, 'would you not have abandoned me if I had not [allowed you to suffer]? Beneath the cross one learns to love, and I do not grant this to everyone, but only to those souls who are dearest to me.'"[1]

"I hope that the Lord is pleased to accept my sufferings in satisfaction for the innumerable times I have offended Him. After all, what is my suffering in comparison to what I deserve for my sins?

"However that may be, for me it is sufficient to know that God wills it, and then I am quite happy."[2]

"Oh, what a wonderful thing it is to become a victim of divine love!"[3]

PRAYER

Heavenly Father, as I meditate on Your boundless mercy that allows Your divine Son to remain always with us in His Real Presence in tabernacles around the world, as I meditate on what He suffered — and continues to suffer — out of love for me, please help me to accept the daily crosses You call me to bear. Help me to trust that You will always be with me, helping me to bear the load. Always remind me that You allow these daily crosses to purify me, to keep me from serious sin, and to draw me ever closer to You. Make me a "victim of divine love." Thank you. Amen.

35
When I See Jesus Weeping

✠

Jesus began to weep.
— JOHN 11:35

$\mathcal{M}$any times throughout the course of his life, St. Pio experienced visions of Christ and even heard Him speak. But Padre Pio was not the only saint to have seen and heard Our Lord. Many of the saints experienced Christ in these ways, including St. Margaret Mary Alacoque of the Sacred Heart of Jesus and St. Faustina of the Divine Mercy.

Jesus' Words as Spoken to St. Pio, as Recorded in Pio's Letter of March 12, 1917:

"'With what ingratitude is my love for people repaid!' said Jesus. 'I should be less offended by them if I had loved them less.... But my heart is made to love. Weak and cowardly people make no effort to overcome temptation, and indeed they take delight in their wickedness.... The souls [whom I have chosen] ... leave me alone by night, alone by day, in the churches. They no longer care about the Sacrament of the Altar. Hardly anyone ever speaks of this Sacrament of Love. Even those who do speak, alas, do so with great indifference and coldness.

"'My heart is forgotten. Nobody thinks anymore of my love, and I am continually grieved. For many people, my house has become an amusement center.'" [At this point, according to Padre Pio's own words, Jesus remained silent, sobs contracted his throat, and He wept.] Then Jesus continued speaking to Pio: "'I behold, my son, the many people who act hypocritically and betray me by sacrilegious communions, trampling underfoot the light and strength which I give them continually. . . .'

"'I need victims to calm my Father's just, divine anger,' continued Jesus. 'Renew the sacrifice of your whole self, and do so without any reserve.'"

St. Pio, in his letter, then said to a priest friend, "I have renewed the sacrifice of my life, and if I experience some feeling of sadness, it is in the contemplation of the God of Sorrows."[1]

PRAYER

Lord Jesus Christ, God of Sorrows, forgive me for neglecting You in the Sacrament of the Altar. Forgive my sins, which have caused You to shed divine tears. From this day forward, I offer You, in reparation for all the sins against your Precious Body and Blood in the Holy Eucharist, my daily sufferings, trials, temptations, disappointments, and sacrifices. May You accept these humble offerings, and may I never cause You to weep again. Amen.

36
Why Worship and Receive Christ in the Eucharist?

So Jesus said to them, "Very truly, I tell you, unless you eat the flesh of the Son of Man and drink his blood, you have no life in you. Those who eat my flesh and drink my blood have eternal life, and I will raise them up on the last day. . . ."

— JOHN 6:53-54

*I*n addition to gaining you the most important gift from God, eternal life, what does your worship and reception of Christ's Body and Blood in the Eucharist achieve? According to Pope John Paul II, everyone *needs* to worship Christ in the Eucharist. The Pope assures us that the Lord waits for each of us in the Sacrament of Love. Pope John Paul urges us to *make* time to meet Christ in the Eucharist, where we can adore Him and contemplate His Real Presence. And we should do this, according to the Pope, with faith and in reparation for the sins of the whole world.[1]

ST. PIO'S WORDS

"Meanwhile, don't cease to recommend this matter to the Lord with greater insistence. Pray and, if you can, get other souls to pray for this also. Receive daily Communion [for this intention]."[2]

"Let our entire lives, our every action, [our supplications before the Blessed Sacrament], and all our aspirations be completely directed toward making reparation for the offenses which ungrateful people continually do...."[3]

"As soon as you are before God in the Blessed Sacrament ... confide all your needs to Him, along with those of others. Speak to Him with filial abandonment, give free rein to your heart, and give Him complete freedom to work in you as He thinks best."[4]

"On leaving the church, you should be recollected and calm. Firstly, take your leave of Jesus in the Blessed Sacrament: Ask His forgiveness for the shortcomings committed in His divine Presence and do not leave Him without asking for — and receiving — His paternal blessing."[5]

PRAYER

Father God, instill in me a lifelong, growing desire to worship and receive Your divine Son in the Eucharist. Thank you for Your unfailing mercy and love which — by the power of your Holy Spirit and Christ's Word spoken through the priest — make Jesus' Body and Blood always present and waiting for me in the tabernacle. Use my own humble presence before the Eucharist to help atone for my own sins, as well as for the sins of the whole world. Amen.

37

No Surer Pledge, No Clearer Sign

✠

But the day of the Lord will come like a thief, and then the heavens will pass away with a loud noise, and the elements will be dissolved with fire, and the earth and everything that is done on it will be disclosed.

Since all these things are to be dissolved in this way, what sort of persons ought you to be in leading lives of holiness and godliness, waiting for and hastening the coming of the day of God, because of which the heavens will be set ablaze and dissolved, and the elements will melt with fire? But, in accordance with his promise, we wait for new heavens and a new earth, where righteousness is at home.

— 2 PETER 3:10-13

When the "day of the Lord" St. Peter spoke about arrives, you and all of God's children will eternally rejoice and give thanks within the "new heavens" and "new earth." But even now, you can experience a taste of that blessed eternity by worshiping and receiving Christ's Body and Blood in the Blessed Sacrament. The Church says, "There is no surer pledge or clearer sign of this great hope in the new heavens and new earth . . . than the Eucharist."[1]

And when the "day of the Lord" arrives — which for you, personally, could be today, tomorrow, or whatever day your own earthly life ends — Jesus will grant you eternal life, simply because you have eaten His living Bread [see John 6:51].

ST. PIO'S WORDS

"This present life is given to us in order to acquire the eternal. . . . Believe me, in order to live happily while on pilgrimage, we must keep before our eyes the hope of arriving at our Homeland [the new Heaven] where we will stay for eternity. In the meantime, we should believe this firmly, because, given that it is God who calls us to himself, He watches how we make our way to Him and will never permit anything to happen to us that is not for our greater good. He knows what we are, and He will extend His paternal hand to us while we are going through rough stretches. . . .

"Live tranquilly, remove from your imagination that which upsets you, and often say to Our Lord, 'Oh God, You are my God, and I will trust in You. You will assist me and be my refuge, and I will fear nothing.' You are not only *with* God, but you are *in* God, and He is within you. What can a child fear in the arms of its father?"[2]

PRAYER

Heavenly Father, thank you for the Eucharist, that surest "pledge" and clearest "sign" of the "new heavens and new earth" that You promise. By the power of Your Holy Spirit, keep the "eyes" of my mind and soul always focused on that heavenly Homeland, by drawing me to yourself in the Real Presence of Your divine Son in the Eucharist. Help me to fully appreciate the one living Bread, the food that will enable me to live forever in Jesus Christ. Amen.

38
By Way of the Cross

✠

Jesus said to him, "I am the way, and the truth, and the life. No one comes to the Father except through me."

— JOHN 14:6

Then he [Jesus] said to them all, "If any want to become my followers, let them deny themselves and take up their cross daily and follow me."

— LUKE 9:23

You *want* to carry your cross and follow Jesus, the Way, but where do you find the strength to do that — and to do it daily? "From celebration [of the Eucharist] to celebration, as they proclaim the Paschal Mystery of Jesus . . . the pilgrim People of God advance," as they follow Christ — who *is* the Way — along the way of the cross, "toward the heavenly banquet, when all the elect will be seated at the table of the Kingdom."[1]

"Having passed from this world to the Father, Christ gives us in the Eucharist the pledge of glory with Him. Participation in the Holy Sacrifice identifies us with His heart, sustains our strength along the pilgrimage of this life, makes us long for eternal life, and unites us even now to the Church in Heaven, the Blessed Virgin Mary, and all the saints."[2]

ST. PIO'S WORDS

"How can you not rejoice at the sight of so many trials to which the good Lord is subjecting you? Isn't the cross certain and infallible proof of God's great love for your soul? . . . So take heart; bless the hand [of your heavenly Father] that afflicts you for the sole purpose of sanctifying you and rendering you similar to His only begotten Son. Don't believe that the Lord is irritated with you and therefore subjects you to such harsh trials. You would be greatly mistaken in this. The Lord wants to test your fidelity. He wants to inebriate you with the cross of His Son. He wants to purify you. He wants to increase your victory and crown.

"Remember and keep well impressed in your mind that Calvary is the hill of the saints. But remember also that, after having climbed Calvary, and after the cross has been erected and you have died on it, you will immediately ascend another mount called Tabor, the heavenly Jerusalem. Remember that the suffering is short-lived, but the reward is eternal."[3]

PRAYER

Heavenly Father, help me — through the grace, mercy, and strength Your Son offers in the Eucharist — to pick up my cross daily and follow Him. And enable me to do all of that with a spirit of generosity, gratitude, peace, and joy. Thank you. Amen.

39

Mary with Her Divine Son in His Passion

✠

When Jesus [hanging from the cross] saw his mother and the disciple whom he loved standing beside her, he said to his mother, "Woman, here is your son." Then he said to the disciple, "Here is your mother." And from that hour the disciple took her into his own home.
— JOHN 19:26-27

Dying on the cross, Christ gave His Mother to you, and He gave you to His Mother. Take her into your "own home" — your heart — and allow her to help you bear your daily crosses. Mary will always lead you to Jesus, who longs to feed you with His Body and Blood in the Eucharist. "In the Eucharist the Church is as it were at the foot of the cross with Mary, united with the offering and intercession of Christ."[1]

"Mary's role in the Church is inseparable from her union with Christ and flows directly from it."[2]

ST. PIO'S WORDS

"Remember what took place in the heart of our heavenly Mother at the foot of the cross. She was turned to stone before her crucified Son, due to the excessive suffering. . . ."[3]

"What a joy it is to serve Jesus in the desert without manna, water, or any other consolation, except that of being led by Him and suffering for Him. May the most holy Virgin be born in our hearts, to bring us her blessings."[4]

"May the clement and holy Virgin continue to obtain for you, from the ineffable goodness of the Lord, the strength to sustain, to the end, so many trials of love, which He bestows on you. . . ."[5]

PRAYER

Dear Lord, draw me into Your Eucharistic Presence, so that I will always be "at the foot of the cross with Mary." There I will obtain from You the grace necessary to sustain me in those "trials of love" that You permit. Amen.

40
Sign and Pledge of His Love

✠

So they said to [Jesus], "What sign are you going to give us then, so that we may see it and believe you?. . . Our ancestors ate the manna in the wilderness; as it is written. . . ." Then Jesus said to them, "Very truly, I tell you, it was not Moses who gave you the bread from heaven, but it is my Father who gives you the true bread from heaven. For the bread of God is that which comes down from heaven and gives life to the world." They said to him, "Sir, give us this bread always." Jesus said to them, "I am the bread of life. Whoever comes to me will never be hungry, and whoever believes in me will never be thirsty."

— JOHN 6:30-35

*E*ven though they had witnessed the miracles Jesus had performed and had heard His sacred words — from his own lips — the crowds who followed Jesus still demanded from Him a "sign" of His love, manna from Heaven. The Church tells us what sign, what pledge of His love, Christ gave them: his Body and Blood in the Eucharist. "In order to leave them a pledge of this love, in order never to depart from His own and to make them sharers in His Passover, he instituted the Eucharist as the memorial of His Death and Resurrection, and commanded His apostles to celebrate it until his return. . . ."[1]

ST. PIO'S WORDS

St. Pio encouraged everyone to trust in God's love, manifested in "the most holy humanity of His Son in the Sacrament of Love."[2]

"Approach Jesus with the confidence of a child because He loves you more than you can imagine. Do not sadden His heart by convincing yourself to the contrary, or by even fleetingly doubting this."[3]

"Draw very close to the heart of this divine Model so that, with your soul already pierced with heavenly love, you can breathe those holy words of the loving soul: 'My beloved is mine and I am his. . . .' "[4]

"Let this divine Love of your heart," continued Pio, "always be on your breast, in order to inflame and consume you with its grace."[5]

"Don't fail to keep yourself present to the eyes of the divine Bridegroom. Let your soul expand before this divine Sun and don't fear its burning rays, otherwise the cocoon will not open, and the beautiful butterfly will not emerge."[6]

"Let us adore God's silence. . . ."[7]

"[And when you cannot be physically in the presence of Christ in the Blessed Sacrament, remember to] fly in spirit before the tabernacle when you cannot go there with the body and there express your ardent desires. Speak to, pray to, and embrace the Beloved of your soul, better than if you had been able to receive Him in sacrament."[8]

PRAYER

Dear Lord, thank you for the Eucharist, the unfathomable sign and pledge of Your love for me. Thank you that — in this world full of doubt, fear, violence, and countless other evils — You have given me the faith to believe that You are truly present — Body and Blood, Soul and Divinity — in the Blessed Sacrament. From You, the Living Water, I can receive every grace and blessing I need to avoid succumbing to this world's temptations and to increase steadily in holiness and love. By Your grace, I will spend the rest of my days — and throughout all eternity — praising, loving, and thanking You — for the sign and pledge of Your love — the Eucharist — so generously given. Amen.

PART VI

For Eucharistic Meditation

Scripture St. Pio Used in His *Letters*

Introduction

✠

By 1968, the year of Saint Pio's death, millions of people revered this priest who bore the stigmata — but many others mocked him. Some newspapers printed scathing reports that claimed Padre Pio "faked" the stigmata and his other spiritual gifts. Even some of the faithful criticized him. At his Masses they would frequently glance at their watches and impatiently tap their toes because they wanted him to hurry through the prayers. But Padre Pio *lived* the Mass, and he often fell into lengthy ecstasies, in love with God present in the Eucharist.

No matter what troubles assailed him, Padre Pio trusted Jesus. To a friend he wrote, "Pay no attention to your path of trial, but I invite you to keep your eyes constantly fixed on He who guides you to the heavenly Homeland. Why should your soul be despondent? Why should you worry whether you reach the Homeland by way of the desert or through [green] fields? . . . Believe me, Jesus is with you, so what do you fear?"[1]

St. Pio certainly did not fear pain and suffering. He welcomed it. Colossians 1:24 epitomizes Pio's views on suffering: "I am now rejoicing in my sufferings for your sake, and in my flesh I am completing what is lacking in Christ's afflictions for the sake of his body, that is, the church."

No matter what trials you face today — or in the future — remember what Padre Pio wrote: "Call to mind the words the divine Master said to the apostles, and which He says to you today: 'Do not let your hearts be troubled'" [John 14:1].[2]

Before the Blessed Sacrament, meditate on the following Scripture verses that were some of St. Pio's favorites, which he often shared in his letters in order to encourage his readers. Before you begin, invite the Holy Spirit to work in your heart and accomplish what St. Paul describes in Hebrews 4:12: "Indeed, the word of God is living and active, sharper than any two-edged sword, piercing until it divides soul from spirit, joints from marrow; it is able to judge the thoughts and intentions of the heart."

Scripture is God's Word, and by the power of Christ's Word spoken through the priest, and by the power of the Holy Spirit, ordinary bread and wine become Christ's Body and Blood, the source of your hope and joy.

Scripture for Eucharistic Meditation

"Come to me, all you that are weary and carrying heavy burdens, and I will give you rest." — MATTHEW 11:28

No testing has overtaken you that is not common to everyone. God is faithful, and he will not let you be tested beyond your strength, but with the testing he will also provide the way out so that you may be able to endure it. — I CORINTHIANS 10:13

"You will be hated by all because of my name. But not a hair of your head will perish." — LUKE 21:17-18

For the LORD God is a sun and shield; he bestows favor and honor. No good thing does the LORD withhold from those who walk uprightly. — PSALM 84:11

Then Jesus, crying with a loud voice, said, "Father, into your hands I commend my spirit." — LUKE 23:46

Every generous act of giving, with every perfect gift, is from above, coming down from the Father of lights, with whom there is no variation or shadow due to change. — JAMES 1:17

Such is the confidence that we have through Christ toward God. Not that we are competent of ourselves to claim anything as coming from us; our competence is from God, who has made us competent to be ministers of a new covenant, not of letter but of spirit; for the letter kills, but the Spirit gives life. — 2 CORINTHIANS 3:4-6

"But whenever you pray, go into your room and shut the door and pray to your Father who is in secret; and your Father who sees in secret will reward you." — MATTHEW 6:6

I run the way of your commandments, for you enlarge my understanding. — PSALM 119:32

If I must boast, I will boast of the things that show my weakness. — 2 CORINTHIANS 11:30

O give thanks to the LORD, for he is good, for his steadfast love endures forever. — PSALM 136:1

He called the crowd with his disciples, and said to them, "If any want to become my followers, let them deny themselves and take up their cross and follow me." — MARK 8:34

"Truly I tell you, unless you change and become like children, you will never enter the kingdom of heaven." — MATTHEW 18:3

My beloved is mine and I am his; he pastures his flock among the lilies. — SONG OF SOLOMON 2:16

My soul languishes for your salvation; I hope in your word.
— PSALM 119:81

...you have held back my life from the pit of destruction, for you have cast all my sins behind your back. — ISAIAH 38:17

There is no fear in love, but perfect love casts out fear....
— I JOHN 4:18

For you love all things that exist, and detest none of the things that you have made, for you would not have made anything if you had hated it. How would anything have endured if you had not willed it? — WISDOM OF SOLOMON 11:24-25

I will seek him whom my soul loves.
— SONG OF SOLOMON 3:2

If any of you is lacking in wisdom, ask God, who gives to all generously and ungrudgingly, and it will be given you.
— JAMES 1:5

"By your endurance you will gain your souls."
— LUKE 21:19

Accept whatever befalls you, and in times of humiliation be patient. For gold is tested in the fire, and those found acceptable, in the furnace of humiliation. — SIRACH 2:4-5

Humble yourselves therefore under the mighty hand of God, so that he may exalt you in due time. Cast all your anxiety on him, because he cares for you. — I PETER 5:6

"Your kingdom come. Your will be done, on earth as it is in heaven." — MATTHEW 6:10

For to me, living is Christ and dying is gain. — PHILIPPIANS 1:21

And Mary said, "My soul magnifies the Lord, and my spirit rejoices in God my Savior. . . ." — LUKE 1:46

We know that all things work together for good for those who love God, who are called according to his purpose. — ROMANS 8:28

My brothers and sisters, whenever you face trials of any kind, consider it nothing but joy, because you know that the testing of your faith produces endurance; and let endurance have its full effect, so that you may be mature and complete, lacking in nothing. — JAMES 1:2-4

For we do not have a high priest who is unable to sympathize with our weaknesses, but we have one who in every respect has been tested as we are, yet without sin. Let us therefore approach the throne of grace with boldness, so that we may receive mercy and find grace to help in time of need. — HEBREWS 4:15-16

"Therefore, I tell you, her sins, which were many, have been forgiven; hence she has shown great love. But the one to whom little is forgiven, loves little." — LUKE 7:47

"Heaven and earth will pass away, but my words will not pass away." — MARK 13:31

Wretched man that I am! Who will rescue me from this body of death? Thanks be to God through Jesus Christ our Lord! — ROMANS 7:24-25

Therefore take up the whole armor of God, so that you may be able to withstand on that evil day, and having done everything, to stand firm. — EPHESIANS 6:13

Cast all your anxiety on him, because he cares for you. — I PETER 5:7

"Now to him who by the power at work within us is able to accomplish abundantly far more than all we can ask or imagine, to him be glory in the church and in Christ Jesus to all generations, forever and ever. Amen." — EPHESIANS 3:20-21

VII

St. Pio's Maxims for Eucharistic Meditation

Introduction

*L*ike a modern-day Solomon, St. Pio always had a power-packed maxim — a morsel of wisdom — to offer anyone who needed his encouragement, advice, or admonition. Before the Blessed Sacrament, the Font of all Wisdom, meditate on the following maxims, which Padre Pio not only spoke and wrote about, but also lived.

St. Pio's Maxims

- ✛ Remember that one thing only is necessary: to be close to Jesus.
- ✛ The Rosary is our weapon against evil.
- ✛ Pray, hope, and don't worry.
- ✛ Do not try too much to overcome your temptations, as this violence would strengthen them. Despise them, but do not dwell on, or become obsessed with, them.
- ✛ When you need me to do something for you, send me your guardian angel with the message, and I'll do what I can to help you.
- ✛ Whoever loves, suffers.

+ Serve God with a joyful spirit because God is the God of joy.

+ Religion is the academy of perfection in which each soul must learn to allow itself to be handled, planed, and smoothed by the divine Spirit.

+ Rise above yourself with frequent ejaculatory prayers and aspirations of the heart which are true, continual prayers.

+ Live in this way: sweet and lovable toward all.

+ Don't lose heart in the midst of your trials. As long as your heart is faithful to Him, He will not give you more than you can bear.

+ Let us always be attached to the cross.

+ Let us die a holy death, which is worth more than a thousand lives.

+ How great and merciful is Our Lord toward those who abandon themselves in Him.

+ God is our Father, so what have you to fear while you are the child of such a Father, through whose providence not even a single hair will fall from your head?

+ You must observe what the divine Master taught His disciples when He sent them out into the world without money, walking sticks, shoes, knapsacks, and with only one tunic. Remember what He afterward said to them, "Did you lack anything?" And they replied that they had not.

+ Consider that you are already on the road to eternity; you have already placed one foot there. And as long as this eternity will be happy for you, why do you worry if these transitory moments cause you to suffer?

+ Keep Jesus Crucified fixed in your heart and all the crosses of the world will seem to you to be roses.

+ Don't be discouraged when you fall, but animate yourself with new confidence and a more profound humility.

+ Never place too much trust in yourself or count excessively on your own strength.

+ Keep on running and don't ever make up your mind to stop, for you know that to stand still on this path [to holiness] is equivalent to retracing one's steps.

+ Throw yourself confidently into the arms of the heavenly Father with childlike trust. And open wide your heart to the charism of the Holy Spirit, who is only waiting for a sign from you in order to enrich you.

+ Continue to do good and to leave the good outcome to Jesus.

+ Remember, if the devil makes a deafening noise, he is still outside and not inside at all.

+ Jesus will always sustain you in everything.

+ Run to the feet of Jesus in the Blessed Sacrament.

VIII

Litany for Eucharistic Meditation

Using St. Pio's Titles for God Found in His *Letters*

Introduction

✠

*I*n order to help people, God blessed Padre Pio not only with the stigmata, but also with the gift of bilocation — the ability to be in two places at one time.

St. Pio also had the gift of perfume. Many times when he wanted people to know that he was praying for them and that God would meet their needs, the people would smell violets, lilies, or roses. In confession, St. Pio had the ability to read a person's soul. If the person concealed sins from him, Padre Pio would reveal them to that person.

God also granted St. Pio the gift of conversion. Countless people returned to Jesus and the Church through Padre Pio's intercession. By Christ's power, he healed the sick in body, mind, and soul. Padre Pio also prophesied. For example, during World War Two, he told the people of San Giovanni Rotondo that no bombs would hit that city. With a foreign-occupied airbase only fifteen miles away, the people refused to believe their padre's prophecy. But when the war ended and no bombs had struck their town, they believed.

Even though God called him to Heaven in 1968, St. Pio *still* exercises his spiritual gifts. Before he died, he often told people that he would be able to do far more for them from Heaven than he could while on earth. The Giver of all of Pio's gifts dwells within the Blessed Sacrament. As a litany, you can use the titles for God that St.

Pio used in his *Letters*. These titles will help you to honor, praise, understand, and adore the Lord of all good gifts.

Litany

Titles for God Found in St. Pio's *Letters*

Lord, have mercy,
Christ, have mercy,
Lord, have mercy.
Christ, hear us.
Christ, graciously hear us.
God, the Father of Heaven, have mercy on us.*
[*Repeat "have mercy on us" after each invocation.]
God the Son, Redeemer of the World,
God the Holy Spirit,
Holy Trinity, One God,
Jesus, Supreme Good,
Jesus, Sun of Justice,
Jesus, Beloved Spouse,
Jesus, Divine Heart,
Jesus, Divine Love of Our Hearts,
Jesus, Crucified One,
Jesus, Omnipotent Love,
Jesus, Supreme King of Our Hearts,
Jesus, Resurrected,
Jesus, Sweet Spouse of Our Souls,
Jesus, Divine Goodness,

Jesus, Our Most Tender Lover,
Jesus, Beloved of Our Hearts,
Jesus, God of Sorrows,
Jesus, Immaculate Lamb,
Jesus, Our Most Sweet God,
Jesus, Divine Helmsman,
Jesus, Son of God,
Jesus, One with the Father and the Holy Spirit,
Jesus, Divine Master,
Jesus, Our Everything,
Jesus, King of Mercy,
Jesus, Our Sweet Savior,
Jesus, Divine Doctor,
Jesus, Heavenly Master,
Jesus, Divine Infant,
Jesus, Child of Bethlehem,
Jesus, Divine Nazarene,
Jesus, Christ Crucified,
Jesus, Heavenly Bridegroom,
Jesus, Divine Majesty,
Jesus, Son of the Sublime Father,
Jesus, Heavenly King,
Jesus, Beautiful Divine Sun,
Jesus, Divine Model,
Jesus, Love Crucified,
Jesus, Divine Tenderness,
Jesus, Babe of Bethlehem,
Jesus, Most High,
Jesus, Dear Redeemer,
Jesus, Our Life,
Jesus, Divine Lover,

Jesus, Good Shepherd,

Jesus, Author of Life,

Jesus, Most Sweet Lord,

Jesus, Our Breath,

Jesus, The Way, the Truth, and the Life,

Jesus, Who Comforts Us,

Jesus, Immense Goodness,

Jesus, Divine Prisoner of the Eucharist,

Jesus, Our Paradise,

Jesus, Our King,

Jesus, Infinite Sweetness,

Jesus, In the Blessed Sacrament,

Lamb of God, You take away the sin of the world, spare us, O Lord.

Lamb of God, You take away the sin of the world, graciously hear us, O Lord.

Lamb of God, You take away the sin of the world, have mercy on us, O Lord.

Lamb of God, You take away the sin of the world, grant us peace.

Amen.

Conclusion:
My Lord and My God!

✠

Like Thomas, have you ever doubted the presence of Christ? If so, you might identify with this Scripture: "But Thomas (who was called the Twin), one of the twelve, was not with them when Jesus came. So the other disciples told him [in John 20:24-25], 'We have seen the Lord.' But he said to them, 'Unless I see the mark of the nails in his hands, and put my finger in the mark of the nails and my hand in his side, I will not believe.'"

The next week, Christ appeared again to the disciples, but this time Thomas was among them. Christ told him, "'Put your finger here and see my hands. Reach out your hand and put it in my side. Do not doubt but believe.' Thomas answered Jesus, 'My Lord and my God!'" (John 20:27-28).

Christ's Real Presence in the Eucharist invites you, too, to reach out your hand and touch Him. "Do not doubt but believe." Like St. Padre Pio often did, kneel before Jesus in the Blessed Sacrament. There, exclaim, "My Lord and my God!"

Sources for Quotes Used

╬

Note to reader concerning St. Pio's three volumes of *Letters* quoted: Except for some minor editing — such as changing "she" to "you" and "his" to "your" so that St. Pio's words include all readers — all of his quotes (taken from *Padre Pio of Pietrelcina's Letters, Volumes I, II, and III*) — are reproduced practically verbatim.

INTRODUCTION
1. *Padre Pio of Pietrelcina's Letters, Volume I*, page 426
2. *Padre Pio of Pietrelcina's Letters, Volume III*, page 452
3. *Padre Pio of Pietrelcina's Letters, Volume I*, page 246
4. *Padre Pio of Pietrelcina's Letters, Volume III*, page 507
5. *Padre Pio of Pietrelcina's Letters, Volume I*, page 408
6. *Padre Pio of Pietrelcina's Letters, Volume II*, page 357
7. *Ibid.*, page 358
8. *Padre Pio of Pietrelcina's Letters, Volume I*, page 212
9. *Padre Pio of Pietrelcina's Letters, Volume III*, page 714

About the Meditations: How and Why to Use Them
1. *Padre Pio of Pietrelcina's Letters, Volume III*, page 178

PART ONE
Introduction
1. *Padre Pio of Pietrelcina's Letters, Volume III*, page 508

First Meditation
1. *Padre Pio of Pietrelcina's Letters, Volume I*, page 427

Second Meditation
1. *Padre Pio of Pietrelcina's Letters, Volume III*, page 51

PART TWO

Introduction

Fifteenth Meditation

Sixteenth Meditation

Seventeenth Meditation

Eighteenth Meditation

PART THREE

Nineteenth Meditation

Twentieth Meditation

Twenty-first Meditation

Twenty-second Meditation

PART FOUR

Thirty-second Meditation

1. *Padre Pio of Pietrelcina's Letters, Volume III*, pages 553-554
2. *Ibid.*, page 713

PART FIVE

Introduction

1. *Padre Pio of Pietrelcina's Letters, Volume III*, page 309
2. Ruffin, C. Bernard, *Padre Pio: The True Story* (Our Sunday Visitor, 1991), pages 237-238
3. United States Catholic Conference, *Catechism of the Catholic Church, Second Edition* (United States Catholic Conference, Inc. — Libreria Editrice Vaticana, 1997), page 377

Thirty-third Meditation

1. *Padre Pio of Pietrelcina's Letters, Volume III*, pages 939-940
2. *Ibid.*, pages 937-938

Thirty-fourth Meditation

1. *Padre Pio of Pietrelcina's Letters, Volume I*, page 382
2. *Ibid.*, page 234
3. *Ibid.*, page 339

Thirty-fifth Meditation

1. *Padre Pio of Pietrelcina's Letters, Volume I*, pages 385-386

Thirty-sixth Meditation

1. United States Catholic Conference, *Catechism of the Catholic Church, Second Edition* (United States Catholic Conference, Inc. — Libreria Editrice Vaticana, 1997), page 348
2. *Padre Pio of Pietrelcina's Letters, Volume III*, pages 108-109
3. *Ibid.*, page 65
4. *Ibid.*, page 89
5. *Ibid.*, page 90

Thirty-seventh Meditation

1. United States Catholic Conference, *Catechism of the Catholic Church, Second Edition* (United States Catholic Conference, Inc. — Libreria Editrice Vaticana, 1997), page 354

2. *Padre Pio of Pietrelcina's Letters, Volume III*, pages 729-730

Thirty-eighth Meditation

1. United States Catholic Conference, *Catechism of the Catholic Church, Second Edition* (United States Catholic Conference, Inc. — Libreria Editrice Vaticana, 1997), page 339

2. *Ibid.*, page 356

3. *Padre Pio of Pietrelcina's Letters, Volume III*, pages 252-253

Thirty-ninth Meditation

1. United States Catholic Conference, *Catechism of the Catholic Church, Second Edition* (United States Catholic Conference, Inc. — Libreria Editrice Vaticana, 1997), page 345

2. *Ibid.*, page 251

3. *Padre Pio of Pietrelcina's Letters, Volume III,* page 195

4. *Ibid.*, page 487

5. *Ibid.*, page 555

Fortieth Meditation

1. United States Catholic Conference, *Catechism of the Catholic Church, Second Edition* (United States Catholic Conference, Inc. — Libreria Editrice Vaticana, 1997), page 337

2. *Padre Pio of Pietrelcina's Letters, Volume III*, page 64

3. *Ibid.*, page 271

4. *Song of Solomon* 2:16

5. *Padre Pio of Pietrelcina's Letters, Volume III*, page 334

6. *Ibid.*, page 321

7. *Ibid.*, page 28

8. *Ibid.*, page 452

PART SIX

Introduction

1. *Padre Pio of Pietrelcina's Letters, Volume III*, page 263

2. *Ibid.*, page 491

Resources

Information About St. Pio for All Who Are Interested in Learning More About Him

National Centre for Padre Pio, Inc., Mrs. Vera M. Calandra, 2213 Old Route 100, Barto, PA, 19504; telephone: (610) 845-2000; fax: (610) 845-2666; e-mail: ncfpp@earthlink.net; web site: www.ncfpp.com

Our Lady of Grace Capuchin Friary, San Giovanni Rotondo, 71013, Foggia, Italy; telephone and fax: (0882) 457584; e-mail: postulazione@vocedi-padrepio.com; web site: www.vocedipadrepio.com

Bibliography

✠

Di Flumeri, Father Gerardo, O.F.M. Cap. *Homage To Padre Pio*. San Giovanni Rotondo, Italy: Our Lady of Grace Capuchin Friary, 1982.

Di Flumeri, Father Gerardo, O.F.M. Cap., editor. *Padre Pio of Pietrelcina Letters, Volumes I and II*. San Giovanni Rotondo: Italy, 1994.

Gaudiose, Dorothy M. *Prophet of the People*. New York: Alba House, 1974.

McGregor, Father Augustine, O.C.S.O. *Padre Pio: His Early Years*. San Giovanni Rotondo, Italy: Our Lady of Grace Capuchin Friary, 1981.

The New Revised Standard Version Bible: Catholic Edition. Tennessee: Catholic Bible Press, 1993.

Parente, Father Alessio, O.F.M. Cap., editor. *Padre Pio of Pietrelcina Letters, Volume III*. San Giovanni Rotondo: Italy.

Parente, Father Alessio, O.F.M. Cap. *Send Me your Guardian Angel*. San Giovanni Rotondo, Italy: Our Lady of Grace Capuchin Friary, 1984.

Ruffin, C. Bernard. *Padre Pio: The True Story (Revised and Expanded)*. Indiana: Our Sunday Visitor, Inc., 1991.

Schug, Rev. John A., Cap. *Padre Pio: He Bore the Stigmata*. Indiana: Our Sunday Visitor, Inc., 1976.

United States Catholic Conference, *Catechism of the Catholic Church, Second Edition*. United States Catholic Conference, Inc. — Libreria Editrice Vaticana, 1997.

Milestones
in St. Pio's Life

✠

1887, May 25 — born in Pietrelcina, Italy

1903, January — enters Capuchin Novitiate in Morcone

1910, August — ordained in Cathedral of Benevento

1918, September — receives the stigmata

1947, May — inaugurates Home for the Relief of Suffering

1968, September 22 — celebrates last Mass

1968, September 23 — dies

1997, December 18 — proclaimed "Venerable"

1999, May 2 — beatification

2002, June 16 — canonization — proclaimed "St. Pio of Pietrelcina"

About the Author

*E*ileen **Dunn Bertanzetti** is the author of other books —
including *Padre Pio's Words of Hope* (Our Sunday Visitor),
Saint Pio of Pietrelcina: Rich In Love (Pauline Books &
Media), and *Molly Pitcher: Heroine* (Chelsea House) —
and more than 150 articles and stories. Since 1989,
through The Institute of Children's Literature, she has
taught adults how to write for publication. Through her
husband, children, grandchildren, family, friends, and the
entire Body of Christ, His Church, Eileen discovers God
loving her — and she is grateful.